Lengthen Your
Leadership Stride

Lengthen Your Leadership Stride

How to Succeed in Your Church Calling

Bruno Vassel III

International Standard Book Number
0-88290-208-3

Library of Congress Catalog Card Number
83-80451

Horizon Publishers Catalog and Order Number
1024

Printed and Distributed in the
United States of America
by

Horizon
Publishers &
Distributors, Inc.

———————————

50 South 500 West
P.O. Box 490
Bountiful, Utah 84010

Dedication

This book is dedicated to my wife, Cari,
and to our five children,
Cayr, Elizabeth, Bruno IV,
Jennifer and Christopher,
for their constant love and support.

Acknowledgments

This book could not have been published without the help of many people. My sister, Mary Hill, author of *Angel Children*, was an unwavering source of encouragement, good ideas, and constructive criticism. She receives a double portion of thanks.

My dear wife, Cari, my parents, Dr. Bruno and Mary E. Vassel, and my sister, Elisabeth Andersen, each made significant contributions as they carefully proofread the manuscript and added valuable ideas, corrections, and constant moral support. Several friends were also kind enough to read portions of the early manuscript.

I am grateful to Horizon Publishers and Distributors, Inc., for their willingness to publish this book, for their many professional suggestions and ideas, and for the time commitment, and quality of work which they produced.

There are many other people who made this book possible through their teachings, time, and example. This list includes mission presidents, many church leaders with whom I have worked, and the teachings and influence of General Authorities, business associates, and many close friends.

Finally, I wish to express my deep love and appreciation to my wife and children for their total support and patience during the long process of writing this book. For all this I am grateful to the Lord and acknowledge His influence in my life and in preparing this book.

Introduction

One of the great strengths of The Church of Jesus Christ of Latter-day Saints is its lay ministry because everyone has a chance to participate in church leadership. Skills required to be successful in church positions improve through experience, observation, trial and error. The purpose of this book is to shorten the time it takes to develop leadership skills.

Through the Prophet Joseph Smith, Jr., the Lord gave instructions to those who were not the twelve apostles, nor the seventy, but who held high and responsible offices in the Church. He admonished them to learn their duty and to be diligent in that which they were called to do. (D&C 107:98-100.) Our Prophet today has continually stressed our need to do what we are called to do better, and faster; to lengthen our stride.

This book blends good business practices with insights and experiences I have gained in branch, ward, stake, and regional positions. These ideas are my own. They should not be considered church policy, but helpful thoughts and suggestions. By applying these ideas, leaders in the Church can significantly lengthen their strides and become successful leaders, now.

Preface

Today's Leadership Challenge

The number of converts to the Church from many parts of the world is truly astounding. Thousands are being baptized every year. There is, therefore, an urgent need for strong leadership. To meet this need, less-experienced members are called to leadership positions. Converts are asked to serve after only a few months in the Church. Recently, for example, I have met bishops in South and Central America with less than two years' membership, stake presidents with less than five. These recent converts fulfill their callings in an exemplary manner, but the challenges they face due to lack of experience are formidable.

This lack of leadership experience is not just confined to converts. Thousands of lifelong members are called each year to serve in church positions for which they have little or no experience. These members also need a faster way to learn to be successful in their church callings.

I am reminded of the first model airplane I built. I used an accurate, detailed blueprint. When the model was completed my boyish mind was proud of the accomplishment. It had two wings, one reasonably straight tail, and seemed strong enough to withstand the bumps and bangings I was sure it would have to endure. My plane never broke: not even a hole in the wing. It never flew, either. The little .049 engine just pulled it around and around in a circle on the ground. I think it had something to do with the twenty-one tubes of airplane glue I used to insure its strength. The wings were almost solid glue! My blueprints were adequate. My experience was not. Many church members today face this challenge pertaining to leadership experience.

Handbooks Are Blueprints

Handbooks of the Church are indispensable to those called to leadership positions. They are the first resource for procedures and policies, job descriptions and for answers to many questions. They are the blueprints upon which to build an organization or carry out our duties while leaving the execution of activities to the individual. But for this reason many a church member, after having read what the handbook says pertaining to his particular calling, may have thought: "I'm anxious to be of service but where do I start? How can I find time to do what seems to be expected of me?"

What To Do and How To Do It

There are two key challenges: *what should we do?* and *how should we do it?* The following chapters deal with what LDS Church leaders should do, coupled with tips showing how to do what we are supposed to be doing. Principles discussed apply to a variety of leadership positions in branches, wards, districts and stakes. Section two will focus on how to develop and use skills needed by leaders throughout their church assignments. The final section of this book discusses four critical factors which form the foundation upon which all principles and ideas must firmly rest in order to achieve the success we want to obtain.

Ideas, suggestions, and experiences presented are the result of my twenty-five years of church involvement in North America, South America and in Europe. Additionally, I have blended in many sound business and management principles gained while owning my own company, and by working on three continents for a multi-national corporation. Part of my professional responsibilities have included overseeing the training and development of leadership skills for over 7,000 employees in several languages. If the ideas found in this book will be applied, neither converts nor lifelong church members will have to go through years of trial and error to become effective church leaders.

Contents

Section I
Getting Started

Chapter 1

Pre-Work

Of the millions of experiences which make up our lives, some are etched into our memories in such a way that they are not easily forgotten. One such instance for me was being called to serve as a bishop. What an emotional and exciting moment when the stake president sat in our home and said, "The Lord, through His living prophet, has called you to be a bishop." Scenes similar to this are repeated many times a day throughout the world as lay members are asked to serve in a variety of important church positions.

When we are given church assignments, the temptation might be to jump right in. Our rationale: "The faster we start the sooner we will be productive." There is a danger here in our lack of understanding the concept of work versus pre-work.

We may think that work produces results but that pre-work does not. We think pre-work comes before we start to do what is important. This misconception comes from the word "pre-work." *Pre* is a prefix meaning "before, in front, or in advance of." We may think that since it "comes before" or "in advance of" the work that "pre-work" is less important. Nothing could be further from the truth. Pre-work is critical if we are to successfully fulfill our church leadership roles.

Exactly what makes up pre-work? To answer this let us look at several activities church leaders should perform. They are specific forms of planning and forethought. They constitute what is called "pre-work."

Strengths and Weaknesses

Each of us has both strengths and weaknesses—areas where we excel and areas where we do not. If we are going to be successful in leadership positions, we must do more than just be aware of our strengths and weaknesses. We must consciously plan to use our strengths and compensate for our weaknesses. Various gifts are given to each of us severally so that we might help each other. The Apostle Paul said, "But the manifestation of the Spirit is given to every man to profit withal. For to one is given by the Spirit the word of wisdom; to another the word of knowledge by the same Spirit; To another faith by the same Spirit; to another the gifts of healing by the same Spirit; To another the working of miracles; to another prophecy; to another discerning of spirits; to another divers kinds of tongues; to another the interpretation of tongues: But all these worketh that one and the selfsame Spirit, dividing to every man severally as he will." (1 Cor. 12:7-11.)

There might be people who think to themselves after reading what Paul said: "Yes, but I don't have exceptional faith; wisdom, knowledge nor the ability to prophesy." That is just the point. Not all of us do possess these specific gifts or strengths. But that does not mean we do not have strong abilities and areas in which we do excel. Some people are great athletes, others have abilities to deal with financial matters, while still others have a unique ability to work with the youth. There are people who are excellent organizers and others who are gifted in following through with details. There are those who have gained insight into the particular needs of single adults or the elderly, while others have that rare ability to keep a little child's attention while teaching a gospel principle.

No one person is gifted in all these areas. What is a strength for one person may not be for another. What is most important is to realize that we each do possess certain abilities. By recognizing this principle we can make better decisions in calling people to work with us, as well as in organizing our own time and efforts more effectively. The results will be better, stronger, more prepared working units in the Church.

Bishop Rodriguez is a good example of one newly called bishop who understood this principle of maximizing one's strengths and reinforcing any weakness. He was a talented accountant. To handle financial matters of the ward would be easy and enjoyable for him. Brother Rodriguez was also a good detailed organizer and capable in following through on assignments and in the use of a calendar for planning. A convert of six years, Bishop Rodriguez did not have much experience in either doctrinal or procedural matters in the Church. And although he loved the youth he knew he was not particularly gifted in working with and motivating them.

To compensate for these areas of weakness, Bishop Rodriguez prayerfully chose a first counselor; an older man who knew LDS Church doctrine and basic church policies and practices. As second counselor the bishop chose a younger man gifted in working with young people; a returned missionary who could also help with the seventies missionary work in the ward. Bishop Rodriguez knew that both these brethren loved the Lord, they they would be loyal to him as bishop, and that they would work hard to fulfill their church callings. This pre-work planning by the newly called bishop would certainly help him as he began his administration.

Each of us must do as Bishop Rodriguez did—we must carefully consider our strengths and weaknesses. We will then be in a better position to organize and plan for success in our church assignments.

What To Do If You Have No Counselors

Even without counselors, yours is still an important assignment which requires leadership skills. Sunday School and primary teachers and teachers of our youth fit into this category as do stake high councilmen, communications directors and many other positions in the Church. What do these people do after they have analyzed their areas of strength and weakness?

Fortunately, leadership in The Church of Jesus Christ of Latter-day Saints is based on those fundamental principles the Savior taught such as love, charity, brotherly kindness, and caring for one another. These attributes are practiced thousands of times a day around the world as Latter-day Saints help one another to be successful in church callings. This help comes in many forms. What is most important is to be aware that it is available to those who recognize they have a need, and then ask others for assistance. An example or two will help clarify how this principle works.

Consider a teacher in a priesthood quorum, Relief Society, a Sunday School class, or in the Primary. The principle is the same in each situation: if the teacher recognizes that to plan or present a lesson is difficult, and if his church unit has the teacher development class to teach these skills, the teacher should attend. There are other ways to learn desired skills. Presidency members, church leaders on the local level, friends, or another knowledgeable teacher in the ward or branch can be asked to assist. It is human nature for us to appreciate recognition by others that we are able to do a particular thing well. Most people would be flattered and pleased to help strengthen another person.

Teachers in the Church who do not improve their skills either do not analyze their areas of strength and weakness or they do not ask for help once they know they have a need. The following scripture, though generally thought of as referring to divine help, also suggests that we will receive help and guidance from others if we will first do our part: "Ask, and it shall be given you; seek, and ye shall find; knock, and it shall be opened unto you: For every one that asketh receiveth; and he that seeketh findeth; and to him that knocketh it shall be opened." (Matt. 7:7-8.) We must ask, seek, and knock in order to receive help.

An example from my own past of how I used help from good friends further shows how we can use pre-work to strengthen our areas of weakness. The first few months of my being bishop were filled with trial and error, experimenting, testing, and learning by my actions and the actions of others.

It started immediately. I had been bishop for only three days when a totally inactive family called with a request that I perform the marriage ceremony for their daughter and future son-in-law. I said I would be happy to help in any way that I could. We set up an appointment to meet and discuss the marriage in detail.

I hung up the telephone feeling very insecure. My first thought was; "Maybe I could call the previous bishop and ask him if he would like the opportunity to do one last marriage." The reality of my situation, however, was very clear. I realized that I was called, ordained, and set apart to be bishop of that ward. It was now my duty and responsibility; I could not delegate that assignment to anyone else.

To have good, faithful, and knowledgeable friends in the Church is extremely important for a number of reasons. One which may not be always obvious is the help they can give us as we are called on to fulfill new and challenging assignments in the Church. Mine, now, was to perform a marriage ceremony. My first step, after rereading what the handbook said, was to get ideas and suggestions from my stake president. Next, I turned to the man who had been my greatest personal teacher in the areas of leadership and church government.

Wendell Archie Bunker was born and raised in St. Thomas, Nevada, a small town now covered by man-made Lake Mead. He came from a humble family, rich in Latter-day Saint Church tradition and leadership strength. During his sixty-plus years he had known and learned from both General Authorities and local church leaders as he served in ward and stake positions. Several years earlier, I had been fortunate to have served as second and then first counselor to Brother Bunker in a Las Vegas ward bishopric. I knew that Bishop Bunker could masterfully perform a marriage and that he would be happy to help me with the one I now faced.

One long distance phone call later I was feeling much better. Brother Bunker had given me many good ideas liberally mixed with wise counsel which I needed. He also promised to immediately mail me excerpts from several marriages he had performed. Thus my first marriage ceremony went smoothly. The young couple and their families seemed pleased. I had the Lord to thank most of all for giving me courage and insight. Also, church handbooks, stake leaders, and dear friends had each played an important pre-work role in helping me to be successful.

Another example of how church members can and do help each other is illustrated by the experience Sister Mary Evans had as a newly called ward Public Communications Director (P.C.D.). The stake P.C.D., Brother McCroy, gave her literature which explained the basics of her calling. Even though the written material was good, it did not contain all the explanations of "how to" which Sister Evans felt she needed. Since Brother McCroy was also new in his calling, he was still learning about public communications himself and he did not have many of those answers for Sister Evans.

Knowing his own weaknesses in this area, the stake public communications director contacted an inactive member of the stake who worked at a newspaper to ask whether he would be willing to meet with him and Sister Evans to help them in his area of expertise: public communications. The knowledgeable journalist-member was obviously flattered by the request. He said he would be happy to answer their questions. By asking an expert for help, both Sister Evans and Brother McCroy significantly strengthened an area of previous weakness. An important by-product of this experience was the positive personal contact and involvement they had with a less active member of the Church.

We have seen that a critical part of getting started in a new church position is to consider our strengths and weaknesses, to maximize our strong points, to reinforce ourselves in areas of weakness. To further prepare for a new church calling, let us consider another important area of pre-work planning and organizing.

Style

The way in which we fulfill our church leadership responsibilities is called "Leadership Style." Our effectiveness is, in a large part, the result of the style we use. Our leadership style communicates our level of expectations to others as well as setting mood, tone and degree of openness in our administration. Thus the style we use in fulfilling our church callings shows those with whom we work what we expect of them. It is important that we become aware of this principle since our style communicates non-verbally to others our expectations and degree of openness. Once formed, these impressions are extremely difficult to change in the minds of others.

This matter of leadership style helps, or gets in the way of, many members who are called to very responsible positions in the Church. Consider two branch presidents: both are faithful, hard-working, experienced members, neither of them willing to compromise on gospel principles. One of the two presidents continually has members wanting to meet with him to discuss everything from marital problems and finances to moral matters and transgressions needing confession. The other branch president rarely has anyone ask to speak to him on such matters.

Why such a striking difference in the reactions by members to these two faithful branch presidents? The primary reason does not lie in a difference of needs on the part of the members in different areas of the world since there are people everywhere who are struggling with financial problems, marital and family problems or with personal problems which range from morality to lack of a strong testimony.

The members' reactions to the two branch presidents has to do with differences in their leadership style. The branch president who had few people come and speak to him on personal matters had a leadership style which communicated two negative feelings to the members: first, he was so busy he would rather not be interrupted and second, that he was too rigid and unforgiving to ever show the compassion members need to go through the confession process in repenting, or in discussing difficult problems. Not that the branch president ever openly told the members he felt this way; he may not have wanted to appear this way. But his actions and his style of handling situations in the branch communicated non-verbally a clear message to the members: "Don't come to talk to the branch president."

By contrast, the branch president who continually had members wanting to speak to him had decided, as he began his administration, that it was very important to appear accessible to the members. To accomplish this, he told them that he was interested in them. By his actions and style of leadership in the branch he showed them that his interest was real. This president visited in the members' homes. He acted interested and concerned. He listened when people talked to him. He was careful not to be too quick to judge or to react harshly when members with problems talked to him and he made a concerted effort to show compassion and patience in his counseling. Certainly the branch president was firm when necessary and he did not compromise gospel principles and standards. But his firmness and his reproof, when called for, were always done in a way that let the members know their president loved them—even the serious sinners—but that he hated the sins. He was practicing the counsel given by the Lord through the Prophet Joseph Smith in Doctrine and Covenants 121:43 when He said: "Reproving betimes with sharpness, when moved upon by the Holy Ghost; and then showing forth afterwards an increase of love toward him whom thou hast reproved, lest he esteem thee to be his enemy."

As we look at the differences in leadership style between these two branch presidents, it would be incorrect to assume that one was born knowing how to be an effective leader while the other was not. Leadership skills are skills which we must learn. Even people gifted in this area had to develop and strengthen their skills. We can all develop a good leadership style, and to do so will greatly enhance our effectiveness as church leaders.

Although the example of the two branch presidents was used, as we have discussed a leader's style, the same principles apply to Relief Society, Primary, or Sunday School presidents and their counselors, priesthood quorum presidencies and group leaders, bishoprics, stake and district presidencies, high councilmen, mission presidents, and all other callings in the Church.

Our Style Determines Productivity In Others

Another important aspect of our leadership style is the definite feelings fostered in those with whom we work which will affect how hard they will be willing to work. Two common sayings explain this principle. First: "You can catch more flies with honey than with vinegar." The application of this is that a gentle, loving leadership style is more effective in the Church than a sour, hard, or rough approach. From time to time you see leaders try to use this rough style. They may be trying to get people to do home teaching or visiting teaching, to work on a welfare project, to do missionary work or to help in building a new church. These approaches often cause members to become frustrated, angry, or just less committed. The second saying is: "You can lead a horse to water but you can't make him drink." If force is not the way to get a horse to drink, or to get members to respond to leaders, what is the answer? The answer is to change our style, our tactics. It is really quite easy to get a horse to drink water: just put a little salt in his oats. In the Church we need to similarly develop a style of leadership which does not force, but which motivates members to want to follow our directions.

A typical situation faced by leaders throughout the Church is the challenge to get members to do home teaching and visiting teaching. One Relief Society president was having trouble getting many of her visiting teachers to visit their assigned families. Her style of handling this situation was to tell the sisters in each Relief Society meeting how poorly they were doing, and that if they did not complete their visiting teaching she would have to do it for them. She also made many members feel uneasy by asking for a show of hands as to who had done their visiting teaching. This kind of leadership style antagonized members and fostered resentment toward both leaders and the visiting teaching program. Going to Relief Society became a chore rather than a pleasure. When sisters did do their visiting teaching it was often for the wrong reasons and with an improper attitude. Under such conditions it was impossible for the program to be successful or to fill the needs of members. It became an ineffective tool in the hands of ward leaders.

Contrast this with the leadership style of Sister Angela Schmidt. There had been problems in the past, but when she was called as Relief Society president she decided to change the situation. Her leadership style was based on hard work, lots of love and patience shown by herself and her counselors, and by the use of a definite action plan.

After meeting and discussing her plans in detail with her counselors and secretary, Sister Schmidt asked that they fast and pray about the plan. They then presented it to the bishopric and asked for support which was enthusiastically given. The next step was to review the ward's records to make sure all sisters age eighteen and over were accounted for.

Sister Schmidt and her counselors arranged family schedules so that they could visit all the Relief Society sisters in the ward. It required major commitments and support from each of her counselor's families and her own, but it also clearly showed sisters in the ward the interest and commitment of their Relief Society presidency. Sister Schmidt reasoned that actions would speak louder than words, and would obtain better results.

As the Relief Society presidency visited in members' homes, they explained the concept of sisterhood where love and concern for one another are most important. Compassionate service was defined in such a way that charity, love and concern for each individual became evident. After bearing a strong, humble testimony of the divinity of the work and gratitude for her new calling, Sister Schmidt asked each sister with whom she visited if she would be willing to help support the Relief Society and strengthen other sisters in the ward. Who could say "no" to such a request?

Sister Schmidt had prearranged for one of her counselors to be prepared to do a visiting teaching survey by asking each member in whose home they were visiting several specific questions. The Relief Society presidency wanted to find out four things: (1) who was doing visiting teaching; (2) the member's general attitude about visiting teaching; (3) whom were they visiting; and (4) helpful information about those families the visiting teacher was seeing. This information would be very helpful later as they considered whether changes in existing visiting teaching assignments were needed. Also, by getting to know Relief Society members better, Sister Schmidt and her counselors could better plan visiting teaching routes, and how to meet individual needs of sisters in the ward.

Sister Schmidt was a strong believer in the power of testimonies. At almost every Relief Society meeting she had a different sister take about five minutes to bear testimony regarding one aspect of visiting teaching; often a teacher with a moving experience she had recently while visiting with one of her families, or a sister who had received help of a special kind. The spirit of true sisterhood, of compassion for one another, and of the joys in service were communicated to everyone present during such testimonies.

Over a period of time, Sister Schmidt asked a number of the sisters to bear their testimonies on this subject. She did not ask this of just the most active sisters; she also gave the opportunity to sisters less well known. It usually worked best if Sister Schmidt told a sister before the meeting that she would like her to relate an experience.

This style of motivating visiting teachers was much more powerful and successful than simply reminding the sisters of their duty each meeting. The principles and style Sister Schmidt used will work equally well for priesthood leaders who work with home teachers. It can also serve as an effective framework for dealing with many other challenging leadership situations in the Church. In summary, we must recognize that the style we use in fulfilling our positions in the Church has a definite impact on our success.

Determining Needs

Inherent in every church position are certain basic needs which must be met in order to successfully fulfill a specific calling. For example, the need exists for a teacher to be present on a regular basis in order to be effective. Another basic need associated with a teacher's calling is the importance of learning course material through proper preparation.

As we begin a new church calling, it is important to identify and write down basic needs associated with that position. Ask the person who called you to the position and the person to whom you will report for ideas as to what the most critical needs are which must be fulfilled. Also carefully review what the Church handbooks say about your particular calling to further identify critical needs of that job.

Besides the basic needs in a church calling, there are other needs unique to each position which might change as circumstances surrounding the position change. It is important to identify these needs and to plan to meet them in order to really be successful.

A good example of this principle is the situation faced by Hugh A. McLean, a former bishop of mine. Our ward in northern New Jersey had been meeting in an elementary school since we did not have a building of our own, nor were there other LDS Church facilities close enough for us to use. We clearly needed our own building. Recognizing this as one of the special needs our ward faced, Bishop McLean spent countless hours on the important project of getting a church building for the ward. The result of his efforts was a lovely new building.

Upon Bishop McLean's release, I was called as bishop of the Fardale Ward. Many of the needs I faced were similar to those faced by the former bishop, but there were also areas I needed to concentrate on which differed from those faced by Brother McLean. Had either of us failed to recognize those unique needs which existed during each of our administrations, we would have been less successful than we were.

There are a number of specific things you can do to help determine what the unique needs are in your particular church calling. Let us consider several aids to help us identify needs.

1. *Records:* One of the most obvious, yet least used sources of finding the specific and unique needs in a church position is records kept which pertain to each church job. Such records include minutes of meetings, agendas, attendance records, written goals and objectives of past administrations, as well as lesson manuals and statistical information.

By reviewing such information sources, a newly called Sunday School teacher would find out who had and had not attended class recently, the students' attendance at other church functions, whether home and visiting teachers had been assigned to each class member, what were identified as important needs in the past, what was done to meet these needs and how effective were those efforts, what lesson topics were emphasized or missed, and which priesthood and auxiliary leaders should be contacted regarding certain students in order to obtain further information.

By reviewing records, a newly called bishop or branch president can determine the activity level of twelve-to-eighteen-year-olds, whether youth presidency meetings and regular interviews with the bishopric and the young have taken place, which youth need special attention, how much priesthood quorums have helped through home teaching, and how effective are adults presently working as youth leaders. He can also determine from the records what is now needed to be emphasized and done to further strengthen the youth.

Church records, then, are a marvelous source of information available to help anyone called to a new church position. These records should be carefully reviewed as part of the pre-work associated with a new church assignment.

2. *Past Results:* As children we loved to retell silly jokes over and over again. One of our favorites was about a man, a swimming pool, and several over-anxious divers. The story went like this. Did you hear about the man who was standing next to a swimming pool? As each person would dive into the pool the man would sadly shake his head and say, "I sure wish it were Saturday today." Finally a

curious spectator asked our friend, "Why do you keep saying that you wish today were Saturday?" To this question the sad man replied, "Because they are going to fill the pool with water on Saturday!" As the punch line was retold, all of the children would laugh and laugh at the ridiculous situation of people who jumped into an empty pool.

Few adults would be so naive as to blindly follow others and jump into a swimming pool without first checking water level, temperature and reactions of those who had already jumped in. We would want to know the results of their actions. Were they all right? Was the pool safe? Based on the results of their actions we would then decide what we intended to do.

Similarly, in newly assigned church jobs, we should find out about results achieved by those who preceded us in our callings before we either follow them or make changes. If we have already been in our present position for some time, we should closely review our own results in order to evaluate our personal effectiveness.

I first began to learn this concept of looking at results to identify needs after several years serving as a bishop's counselor. Our youth programs seemed to be the envy of the stake as we took the youth on one interesting activity after another. We thought that by involving the young people in exciting and diverse activities they would be more interested in participating in church. It was also hoped that good associations with other Latter-day Saint youth and adults would further help teen-agers to develop testimonies of the gospel.

After about three years, the bishopric and other adults working with the young people began to realize that there were some basic problems with the programs for young men and young women. Our results were not what we expected or wanted. We were losing too many youth to inactivity, immorality, and indifference instead of their having strengthened testimonies. The oldest teen-agers were not going on missions or getting married in the temple.

By carefully studying results we were obtaining, it was possible to identify several needs which were not being met. The youths' needs of strengthened testimonies were not being satisfied by merely providing them with activities such as swimming, hiking and basketball any more than a country club would have filled these religious needs. Also, the critical need for parental support and involvement was lacking, as well as the basic requirement in successful church youth programs that activities be a coordinated part of a total, religiously oriented plan; that activities should not become the whole program.

Changes were made in our ward's youth programs based on a careful analysis of our prior results. We looked at the most important needs our youth had and put more emphasis in those areas while encouraging parental involvement as much as possible. Certainly there were interesting and fun activities but we made church-related goals part of the requirements in order for the youth to be able to participate in these activities.

There were other things we did to improve our youth programs. The important point here is to recognize that no matter what position you occupy in the Church (whether in a bishopric, as youth leader, teacher or in a stake) the principle of reviewing past results can significantly help you to be more efficient in fulfilling church callings.

3. *Staff Needs:* No discussion of determining needs would be complete without including a section specifically related to the staff with whom we will work in our church callings. We must make sure that the needs of these people are identified so that our planning will include specific actions to meet their needs.

This principle of determining staffs' needs becomes clearer when we recognize that calling people to positions in the Church fulfills two important functions. The more obvious reason is that the many jobs which exist will be filled. The second reason people are asked to serve is for their own development. This great principle of providing an opportunity for every member to actively participate and thereby learn and develop skills and abilities is a testimony to the inspiration behind the Latter-day Saint organization.

There are thousands of people among those who join the Church every year who say to themselves, "I could never stand in front of a congregation to say a prayer or give a talk. To be an effective teacher or to run an organization like the Relief Society or a full ward is completely out of the question." But just a few years later many of these members serve in diverse positions in stakes and districts throughout the world. Whether they serve effectively depends on the extent to which their church leaders help them meet their development needs.

It is important for us to catch the vision of how significant our role is in helping to teach others that which we have been taught. As we build and develop people with whom we work, our own work load will be lightened and go more smoothly with their help. We will also enjoy the satisfaction of truly helping our brothers and sisters to grow in the gospel of Christ.

Chapter 2

Priorities

One of the most important tasks anyone faces as he begins a new church assignment is the setting of priorities.

Simply stated, priority setting means to put in order of importance various things we need to do. By going through this process we recognize that some of what we must do requires immediate attention. Other items can wait a little while. The rest are of less importance now. This process is not just critical to achieving initial success in our church jobs. As long as we hold a position of responsibility, whether in the Church, the home, or at work, our success will depend to a large extent on our ability to continually set proper priorities, and then to make sure that we do the most important things first.

The paragraph you just read contains a fundamental success formula which always works when properly applied. There aren't too many prescriptions around with that kind of guarantee, so let's take a few minutes to discuss this one in more depth.

As you review the important steps in this chapter, be careful not to let very human reactions get you into trouble. There are people who hear about these easy steps and who think to themselves: "That is both simple and obvious. I already do some of it anyway." With that thought they do not follow the steps and they are not very successful. Make sure you don't fall into this trap as we look at interdependent principles which deal with priorities.

Make a List

If you are going to be successful in handling a number of priorities simultaneously, you have to make a list of all the various things which need to be done: Not several lists of church-related items; not on scraps of paper; just one complete list to which you add all new priorities as they arise. This list is the first important step necessary in order to handle effectively the many tasks involved in a challenging church job.

If we were to peek at a stake president's priority list we might find: prepare a stake conference talk for the 15th; call Brother Anderson's bishop regarding possible temple-interview problems; prepare for presidency meeting on the 9th; call regional representative about the welfare farm; follow up with executive secretary about my next two weeks' schedule; meet with my first counselor and stake P.C.D. about presenting the mayor with a family home evening manual; call Bishop Lewis about his ward's finances; prepare talk for meeting with missionaries; decide on new high councilman to replace Brother Paul; meet with second counselor and decide on stake Primary reorganization; review high council recommendation for changing ward conference format—and on, and on. It is obvious that a written list is the only way for a busy person such as this stake president to keep track of his many church responsibilities.

Some may say that a list is necessary for people like stake presidents, bishops, and other key leaders but not for less complicated church positions. They might say that those who hold positions such as secretaries or teachers do not require a list of activities or priorities in order to be successful. For example, people with a teaching assignment might feel that all they need to remember is to prepare a lesson every week.

To answer this let's go to Sao Paulo, Brazil, and take a quick look at the priority list of Sister Maria da Silva, an excellent Sunday School teacher. Her list includes: contact Luis (a class member) and have him prepare a portion of the lesson for the 18th; call home and visiting teachers of Cristina and set up a meeting to discuss her lack of attendance; ask the activities committee to get a specialist to help with a difficult lesson for the 25th; review class members' birthdays for next month; contact Joao's father to thank him for participating in last week's class; ask Sunday School president about a larger classroom; review class attendance records to identify problem areas; review next 8 lessons and identify special needs or problem areas— and on and on—all this without even looking at Sister da Silva's list of non church-related activities; things pertaining to her home and family. Can you see why she is such a good teacher, and how a church-priorities list helps her so much?

Experience has shown that all who have a church assignment need an updated list of things they should be doing. This list might include activities which pertain to their church job as well as those which pertain to their family. Many leaders prefer a priority list which will focus on just the church calling. They then have a list for their family and one for their profession. Regardless of the method, to make a list of the many things we need to do in our church callings is very important to our success.

Use List As Your Memory

At this point do not worry about which activity comes first. Just write down everything you can think of that you need to do. Each time you think of something, or are asked to do a church-related activity, write it on your list. In that way, your list will always contain everything you need to be doing—you won't forget anything. Memory listing alone will help many people to become much more effective leaders.

Calendar

Before we give thought to the second principle related to priorities, let's take a minute to mention the effective use of a small pocket calendar. A calendar is not a list. To be a really good leader you need both a list of activities and a calendar.

The calendar is used to remind us of dates, times, and places specific activities will take place while a priority list refers to what we need to do—often to get ready for calendar dates, times, and places. It does little good to prepare for a meeting at church next Thursday evening if you forget to attend. A calendar helps avoid such oversights by reminding us of each day's plans. Likewise, the calendar may show a leadership meeting we should attend, but it will not show the five or six things we need to do in order to properly prepare for that meeting. What reminds us to do those specific things is our priority list.

The first step, then, in properly setting priorities and accomplishing the important activities of our church jobs is to make a detailed list of all we need to do. It also means that we will continually add new items as they arise and that we will keep a small pocket calendar for dates, times, and places of meetings and other activities.

Before going on, stop reading for five minutes. Get a piece of paper and write down all the activities you can think of which relate to your church job. It is important to do this now since the next step will require that you use your list. Please get the paper and pencil and start writing. I'll wait!

Need Some Help?

Some people are able to write down fifteen to twenty-five separate activities immediately. Others will write down one or two and then get stumped, unable to think of anything else. If you are having trouble, the usual reason is that you have written things which are too general and which may cover several individual activities. For example, a certain elders quorum president, with this problem of being too general as he wrote down priorities, had a list with only three items: improve home teaching; visit all the members; get all prospective elders advanced to elders. These are fine activities, but they are much too general. He has to be more specific. There are at least fifteen individual things this elders president might need to do just to get home teaching going: meet as a presidency to discuss home teaching; review records; look at the existing routes, and so on. (Check example of good visiting teaching on pages 24 through 26.)

If you have trouble listing activities, take each priority on your list and break it into at least five different parts. In some cases, you will be able to think of many more things to do than just five. The secret is to break each thing you have to do into as many individual parts as possible.

With a good list of activities written down you are now ready to move on to principle number two in the proper handling of priorities.

Decide Importance Of Each Item On Your List

If you were stuck on the moon sixty kilometers from your space ship, and had to walk that distance to safety, what five things would you want to have with you? That was the question asked to each Master of Business Administration student at Brigham Young University as we started a three-day seminar which began our Masters program.

The professor gave each of us a list of about fifty items ranging from food, a rope, water, matches, a compass, an ax, and oxygen, to a fishing pole and even a pistol. We were told to pick the five most important things to take on our imaginary trek back to safety.

It was immediately obvious that some items on the list were much more important than others. Their priority, at that place and time, was much greater than that of other items. The oxygen and water (in drinkable moon-canteens of course) were the two most critical items since they were necessary to sustain life. The next most important item was the direction finder which would indicate the way back to the spaceship. The fishing pole, matches, ax, and snowshoes were of far less importance on the moon. (They would have been excellent if we had been stranded in snowy Canada or Sweden.)

The example in graduate school clearly showed us that not each item on the moon survival list had the same importance, or priority. The same situation exists with our church callings. Some activities on our list have a higher priority than others. Realizing this, the second principle in the proper handling of time and priorities is that we recognize, and identify, the relative importance of each item on our activities list.

Rating Importance

The easiest and best way to quickly determine the importance of each item on your list is to ask yourself, "How important is it that this item be done now?" You are not asking how important it will be in a week, or a month, but *now*. If you answer your question with "Extremely important now" then put the number one (1) to the left of that activity. If your answer is something like "Not critical but it is important" put the number two (2) at the left of the item. And if your answer as to the importance of an item is "Not very important right now" put the number three (3) to the left of the activity. By doing this you have quickly and easily determined the relative importance of each item on your priority list.

There are activities which can trick us as to their importance right now: they are not due today or tomorrow. They may not even take place for a week or two, but they do require that preparatory actions be started now. You can't always wait until the last minute and be well prepared. An example of this might be the stake conference talk that the stake president had to prepare. Even though he still had two weeks to prepare, it probably required that he start now in order to deliver the message in a truly impactful way. The president would therefore rate that item as a "2" priority—or possibly even a "1"—but certainly not a "3" if much work was still required.

Some people have trouble rating activities on their lists because everything seems important; every item is rated a "1." Should this happen, say to yourself: "Even though they are all important, some of these activities take precedence over others. Some must be done first." Then ask yourself: "Which ones are the most critical to be started right now?" Force yourself to decide and then give those most crucial a "1" rating; the others a "2" or "3." By doing this you are not reducing the eventual importance of anything, just the *relative importance of right now.* Make sure, therefore, that no more than a third of your list of activities are rated as "1" in priority.

Ratings Change

Ratings can change, and they should over a period of time. Something I put on my priority list a month ago may not have been very important then, but I needed to remember it for the future so I wrote it down and put a "3" next to it. Today, as I review my list, I need to change the "3" rating on that activity to a "2." By next week that same item may still be a "2" or it may have become a "1" in importance. By reviewing my priority list every day, I keep the rating of each item current.

One of the nice things about this system of keeping track of activities and rating them as to their importance is that it is flexible: you can change anything you want to, any time you want to, in order to better meet your current needs. Through this simple process your priority list becomes a really effective leadership tool in your hands.

Before going to the third step in successfully dealing with priorities, take a minute and rate the importance of each item on your activities list. Place a "1," "2," or "3" to the left of each item. You should repeat this process of rating the priority of each item at least once every day. It is easy, fast, and crucial to your success as an effective leader.

Success Comes By Doing the "1"s

Let's go back to the moon, 60 kilometers from our lunar lander, and assume you have just finished making a list of many possible items, and also rated them as to their importance right now. There is a "1," "2," or "3" to the left of each item. Such things as oxygen, water, and the direction finder you rated with a "1" as to priority. The fishing pole, snowshoes, and matches were each given a "3" rating. To decide which things you will select for use right now is quite simple: Pick the oxygen and the other "1" rated items. In real life the choosing of priorities should not be any more difficult: Always to the "1" priority items first. Unfortunately, we seem to like to pick less important items rated "3." By doing so we waste time on things which are not important right now. That limits our success.

Don't Do "3"s

Priority "3" items trap us for at least two reasons. First, as we look over our list which may have fifteen or more activities, there are items we either like to do better than others or which are easier. When we do a "3" rated item we make the mistake of thinking that since the activity is on our priority list it has to be done sometime, so why not now? We fail to remember that the "1" rating means the item is critical now while "3" priority means that the activity is of too little importance to be done now. The key to success is to do the important things first: the "1" rated priorities.

Big Projects, Little Pieces Of Time

The second reason that "3" rated priorities trap us into doing them first has to do with *big* projects and *little* pieces of time.

There are important things we need to do in our church callings which require several hours, days, or even weeks of preparation time. To prepare a talk or lesson, reorganize a quorum or auxiliary, write the script for a play, develop a new membership program, or plan a realistic stake budget are a few examples of numerous time-consuming activities we often do to fulfill our callings. The challenge comes because we usually don't have several uninterrupted hours of time for these time-consuming activities. Because our lives are made up of small blocks of time, with many interruptions, we think: "I only have fifteen minutes right now and the "1" rated items on my priority list require several hours of work." The "3" priority items then trap us as we rationalize: "I will do this "3" rated item which should only take ten minutes or so, then I can cross if off my list."

Have you ever fallen into this trap and done a "3" instead of a "1" priority? I would like very much to have a dollar for every time I have made that mistake. It is not difficult to see why. The main reason is because we don't understand how to eat an elephant. You remember how to eat an elephant, don't you? Take one bite at a time! By applying this principle to time-consuming priorities we will do important things first, and do them within the time we have available.

How to Handle Lots of "1"s

To always have several "1" rated items on your list is a natural problem. It usually happens that way, so what do we do and where do we start? The answer is simple. Ask yourself: "Which of these "1" rated items is the most critical to be done first?" Force yourself to choose that most crucial activity then, next to that item, put a "1-A." The "A" means it is the most important "1" rated item right now for you to be working on. The second most important gets a "1-B," and so on. Then start with the "1-A." This system can work wonders in helping you deal with time and priority pressures.

We have discussed the three steps necessary in order to properly deal with priorities. First, make a list of all possible activities or important items. Add to that list as new items arise. Second, identify the present importance of each item by placing a "1," "2," or "3" to the left of each activity on your list, and then rate the "1"s with an "A," "B," "C" and so on to further identify which item is most important for you now. And third, you always spend your time working on "1-A" rated priorities.

There are two other very important principles which effective church leaders have learned to use as they manage their time and deal with priorities. The next two chapters in this section will deal with these ideas. Continue reading: it's a "1-A" priority.

Chapter 3

Delegation

Recently I was in Venezuela on business, working with a high-level director. He has been active in business for over thirty years, yet he continues to have difficulty managing his time and the many priorities he faces every day. His problem is the same as that faced by many church members who are in leadership positions: a failure to delegate effectively.

As Fernando and I talked about the importance of his keeping a list of what he needs to do—prioritizing various activities, then doing the "1" rated items first—he made a comment which is often expressed by people who have trouble managing their time. He said, "My problem, Bruno, is that if I make a list of activities it just frustrates me since there are always at least five or six important things I need to do right now. Each is rated one in priority." Fernando then went on with frustration in his voice. "I just can't do more than one thing at a time, so forget the list; I just work as hard and as long as I can to get it all done."

Unfortunately, Fernando is not "getting it all done." Furthermore, his doctor recently told him that his headaches were due to high blood pressure probably caused by his constant worry about things he is not getting done. I am convinced that proper delegation can help eliminate many such worries, not only for my business associate, but for all who are in positions of leadership. To better understand how this is possible, let's examine Fernando's dilemma and what he could do about it: principles which will work for you as you try to handle priorities better through delegating.

My Venezuelan business friend said that the problem with a priority list is that it shows him five or six "1" rated items and since he can't do more than one thing at a time he gets frustrated and feels an increase in pressure. My answer to this may upset people who have practiced this Fernandian philosophy, but here it goes anyway:

I say nonsense! The problem has nothing to do with a priority list, and little to do with having several "1" rated activities to do simultaneously. It has to do with our reluctance or our inability to delegate. Before getting discouraged, though, remember that some very impressive people have had the problem of not delegating. Let's look at one in particular.

What would you think of a leader who had over a million people leave their homes to follow him into a new country? Not only that, but the Lord performed all kinds of miracles through this man: not just quiet little miracles but really big, impressive, monumental miracles. You would think that such an important leader and prophet would be gifted in handling a number of "1" rated priorities simultaneously through delegation, wouldn't you? Well, Moses was not talented in this area. In fact, this leader was so ineffective that his father-in-law, Jethro, had to step in and explain to Moses how to delegate. Moses had been spending every day trying to deal with the problems of every Israelite who felt like talking to him. (That sounds like some bishops I've met.) Jethro said to Moses, "What is this thing that thou doest to the people? Why sittest thou thyself alone, and all the people stand by thee from morning unto even?" It does not sound like Jethro thought the people were happy about standing in line all day. "And Moses said unto his father-in-law, Because the people come unto me to inquire of God: When they have a matter, they come unto me; and I judge between one and another, and I do make them know the statutes of God, and his laws." Jethro then tells Moses why what Moses is doing is not a good idea. "And Moses' father-in-law said unto him, The thing that thou doest is not good. Thou wilt surely wear away, both thou, and this people that is with thee: for this thing is too heavy for thee; thou art not able to perform it thyself alone." After telling Moses that he is to teach and guide the people, Jethro explains how this is to be accomplished. "Moreover thou shalt provide out of all the people able men, such as fear God, men of truth, hating covetousness; and place such over them, to be rulers of thousands, and rulers of hundreds, rulers of fifties, and rulers of tens, And let them judge the people at all seasons." (Exodus 18:14-18, 21-22.)

The message to Moses that he must delegate could not have been clearer.

Later in the same chapter of Exodus we learn that Moses did follow the wise counsel of his father-in-law. He set up a very efficient system, through delegation, to handle the needs of the people. Moses divided the multitude into groups and assigned leaders to oversee the needs of each group. These leaders were then given the authority necessary to function in their respective positions. The brilliance of Moses as a leader in this example was not that he had a father-in-law who saw the need to delegate: It was Moses' willingness to accept Jethro's wise counsel and to do something about it.

Little Success Without Delegation

We may not be asked to lead a million people as was Moses, but the Lord still expects us to get the job done effectively and efficiently, while we also provide training for other people. In most cases it is impossible to do this without delegating.

A vivid example which taught me the need to delegate came from my dear friend and former bishop, Wendell A. Bunker.

Brother Bunker retired in 1969 following a successful career which included owning his own real estate business. He and his wife, Marion, planned to move from Las Vegas, Nevada, to a cattle farm in southern Idaho Wendell had purchased. The Bunkers sold their lovely home and rented a small apartment while they made final preparations to move.

The Lord has a way of directing our lives, which we usually recognize and fully appreciate only in retrospect. This was clearly the case with the Bunkers' move to an apartment within the Las Vegas 16th Ward boundaries. The ward was made up of over 970 members with less than twenty percent active. There were some choice, dedicated Latter-day Saints in the 16th Ward, but not nearly enough to divide the ward, or to properly staff the existing church unit. The handful of active priesthood holders clearly needed additional help. That help came as the Lord called Brother Wendell Bunker to be bishop of the 16th Ward. Though surprised almost to the point of shock, Brother Bunker accepted the calling and remained in Las Vegas for several years.

In early 1970, my wife, our oldest daughter and I moved to Las Vegas and into an apartment in the 16th Ward. Within a short time Bishop Bunker asked me to serve as his counselor in the bishopric. It was during that time that he taught me the absolute necessity for church leaders to delegate all that they rightfully can in order to be successful.

Bishop Bunker sat down with me and, with emotion, said: "Brother Vassel, it is not just by chance that you moved into this ward." The bishop continued. "I have tried to do this job mostly by myself, spending full time at it. I am putting in twelve to fourteen hours per day all week long, yet the work is not progressing satisfactorily." Brother Bunker then stated a true principle which impressed me greatly. "I have learned that it is not meant for one person to run the ward all by himself." It is so important for us to learn this truism as we strive to succeed in our church callings.

As I have served in various church positions I have often thought back to that talk with Bishop Bunker. His experience taught me that even a talented businessman and leader could not single-handedly do all that needed to be done, regardless of the amount of time spent in trying. It became clear that doing our church jobs single-handedly was not the answer. That is not the way our Heavenly Father wants the Church to be run. We must learn to delegate if we are to become effective church leaders. There is no other way.

Church Callings Require Delegation

God calls us to church positions for two distinct reasons. By understanding this we will also more clearly see why delegation plays such an important role in our being effective in positions of responsibility. The two reasons are (1) to get the job done, and (2) for the members' growth and development.

Arguing which of these is more important is no more productive than debating whether faith or works is more important in helping us return to Heavenly Father. The scriptures make it indisputably clear that we need both faith and works. Likewise, to get the job done, and to train and develop ourselves and others is necessary if we wish to fully magnify our church callings. In fact, it is often physically impossible to achieve one goal without the other.

There are people who have difficulty recognizing this principle: the training and development of church members is as important as getting the work done. Typical examples may include the Relief Society president who makes all the decorations herself for an opening social to show the sisters how it should be done. There are bishops and branch presidents who spend countless hours counseling with people on marital, financial, testimony, and educational matters instead of delegating to other people, and handling the moral problems as they should, or teachers who give every lesson like a lecture, with little class participation or assistance from class members.

In each situation there are people who could and should be called on to assist. By not asking other people to share the work load, what are these leaders communicating to those with whom they work? Counselors, teachers, priesthood leaders, class members, new converts, and less active members are indirectly being told that they are not important. Training and development do not take place. Furthermore, remembering back to earlier discussions on leadership style, we recognize lack of delegating to be one of the weakest leadership styles we can use if we wish to motivate those with whom we work.

Before leaving the topic of delegation, there are other important concepts which must be understood if we are to have success in delegating to others. I refer to accountability and authority.

Authority and Accountability

Authority must be delegated; accountability must not. This is a rule leaders must follow to be successful as they delegate to others. Because this is so important, let's look more closely at what it means. The first part of this rule states that sufficient authority must be delegated from you to the person or persons you are asking to do something for you so that they can successfully complete their assignments. This may sound simple and obvious, but it is frequently not done.

Stake high councilmen are sometimes faced with this problem. There are stake presidencies who give their high councilmen assignments to fulfill, yet when the high councilmen try to carry out their plans they find that their stake presidencies continually want to step back in and do it themselves, their own way. Some brethren spend hours in high council meetings, discussing and developing plans and programs, only to have stake presidencies say: "No, we will do it a different way." They really had not delegated the authority for these high councilmen to do anything except meet together and talk, which is a terrible waste of time.

A better approach for the stake presidency would be to say: "We authorize you, as a high council, to develop and implement a new program within the following guidelines." The presidency would then mention those factors which they felt had to be part of the program. The high councilmen would then have understood what they were not authorized to change. Importantly, they would have also understood that, within those set limits, they were given authority to develop and implement their own ideas and plans. This approach saves time, eliminates duplication of efforts, and keeps everyone much more motivated.

Another example which can show a lack of understanding regarding the importance of delegating authority involves bishops, branch presidents, and priesthood leaders. Too often bishops and branch presidents feel overworked, especially due to the amount of time they spend counseling with members. They may wish that their priesthood leaders would help lighten the load by doing more work and fulfilling their assignments better. This problem is a classic example of the problems leaders can have when they don't delegate authority.

Bishops and branch presidents are clearly told that they are not to do all the counseling in their units . . . and there is always a lot to do! They are directed to delegate everything, except matters related to moral problems, to their priesthood leaders. Yet there are bishops and branch presidents who continue to meet night after night, week after week with their members on marital, financial, testimony, word of wisdom, tithing, and emotional problems. Through these actions, they show that the authority to do such counseling was never given to their priesthood leaders. When this happens, the priesthood leaders remain less effective, while the bishops/branch presidents continue to be overworked and also, most assuredly, less effective.

Now let's look at accountability. I mentioned earlier that sufficient authority must be delegated, but overall accountability must not. Whenever I think of this principle . . . that accountability can not be delegated . . . I think of our youth programs in the church, especially in recent years. But before we discuss accountability in the youth programs, let's define and explain the principles which surround the topic of accountability.

(You may want to read this paragraph slowly!) For each job, whether inside or outside of the Church, there are certain duties, responsibilities, and activities which define the scope and purposes of that job and which also make each job distinct from every other position. When we accept a specific job or calling we automatically become accountable for those duties, responsibilities, and activities which, by definition, make up that position. This means that we must answer to someone, or account for the results of our job, including both the successes and the failures. This accountability for our calling absolutely cannot be delegated. It remains with us as long as we hold the position.

The ultimate person to whom we must answer and account for our particular stewardship is the Lord. There is no delegating that! Additionally, good leaders who preside over us will require that we regularly report to them, with specific information indicating how well we are carrying out our duties, responsibilities, and activities. The serious mistake some leaders make is this: as they properly delegate the necessary authority to others, they think they have also passed the accountability from themselves, for the success or failure of the job, to another person, or persons. As we just learned, you can't pass accountability to others: it's yours to keep until you are released from your church calling.

Misunderstandings which concern the nontransferability of our accountability can be caused by one word: The word is "responsibility." We get into trouble because we say that we gave others the responsibility for doing certain things. There is nothing wrong with giving others responsibility because this really goes hand in hand with giving them the necessary authority to fulfill their callings.

It is perfectly correct to say, "I am giving you the responsibility to do this project. It's all yours." In fact, this makes the person feel important, and responsible, which shows good leadership style on your part.

The important point to remember is that responsibility and accountability are not synonymous. We may give others the necessary authority and the responsibility, but we are still ultimately accountable for the results. Stated another way, we always remain answerable regardless of what we have given others to do.

Youth Programs and Shadow Leadership

Now let's get back to the youth programs. For years and years adult leaders who worked with the youth kept almost all authority and responsibility, and also accepted accountability, to successfully plan and implement youth programs in the Church. This program was the Mutual Improvement Association.

More recently it was felt that additional youth would remain active if youth leaders did two things: First, the leaders needed to focus on the needs of each individual young person rather than on the group as a whole; and second, leaders needed to involve young people much more in planning and execution of the full youth program.

Youth who are leaders are given the necessary authority and responsibility in order for them to plan and implement their own programs and activities.

This new focus is, without question, inspired. In fact, I think it is brilliant! Yet some people might ask; "Then why are some wards and branches struggling with their youth programs?" The answer is made up of many parts, but let's deal now with what seems to be the biggest reason.

A major emphasis of the new youth program is that young people become more involved in both planning and implementing their activities. This is accomplished by giving youth who are leaders the necessary authority and responsibility. Here is where the problem arises: Adult leaders need to remember that they are still accountable for the success of the overall youth program. There are adult leaders who have been called to work with the youth under this new program who do not understand the principles of delegation very well. As a result they are mixing concepts of responsibility, authority, and accountability; especially accountability.

A contributing factor to this confusion has been the misunderstanding of a good idea called "shadow leadership" which means that adult leaders step back and let the youth do their own planning, directing, implementing, and following-up. For shadow leadership to be effective adult leaders must accept their continuing accountability for the success of the programs. They must provide clear assistance, training, counsel and support to the youth such as class and quorum presidents who are the leaders. Without this support by adult leaders, it is not shadow leadership they provide: it is no leadership at all. In such cases the obvious result will be a mediocre youth program at best.

Shadow leadership does not mean that adults do everything for the youth; this is what sometimes happened under the old MIA program. Nor does it mean that adults should step away and let the youth sink or swim.

Let's look at an example of how adult leaders properly used good shadow leadership and delegated to the youth, yet maintained accountability for the success of a youth activity.

In planning a calendar for youth activities for the next six months, the youth who were quorum and class leaders had scheduled one combined activity involving mia-maids, laurels, teachers, and priests per month. (Shadow leadership stepped in and suggested this.)

The first joint activity the youth wanted was a Saturday of canoeing and picnicing. (Shadow leadership then suggested that such an activity would cost money which the youth should earn, not get from their parents. Therefore it might be a good idea to plan a combined fund-raising activity prior to the canoe trip.) The youth accepted that idea and discussed various ways to raise money. They finally decided to have a car wash which was scheduled a month prior to the canoe trip. (Shadow leadership stepped back in at this point and suggested a class or quorum be made responsible for each activity.) The youth assigned the teachers quorum to be in charge of planning the car wash. Priests and laurels were to be jointly responsible for canoe and picnic activities.

As the adult leaders of the youth subsequently met together, they discussed ways they could help the teachers quorum presidency be successful in planning the car wash. The teachers quorum advisor said that he would suggest to the president of the quorum that the planning of the car wash be placed on the quorum presidency meeting agenda in order for plans and assignments to be made. He also suggested to the quorum president that he let the ward's activities committee know what was being planned so that they could help wherever appropriate.

True shadow leadership is that which leads to real success both for the youth and for their leaders. Further, where appropriate, parents of the youth should be involved in order for them to help their children to follow through and thereby be successful.

In summary, our youth need adult leaders who understand their own accountability for the success of the Church's youth program and who are willing to cast a shadow large enough to insure that success. For those of us who are in such positions, it might be helpful to put a card or a sign on our mirror, desk, or refrigerator which says: "We remain accountable."

In this chapter we have spent quite a bit of time discussing delegation since it is so important to our success as church leaders. There is one other important aspect of church leadership which we have not yet discussed, and which must be considered whenever we begin a new church calling. It becomes a significant issue every time we receive a calling, yet many people struggle with it throughout their lives. Due to its importance, we will end Section I by developing some positive ways to resolve this issue which is how we handle other important responsibilities in our lives while actively filling our church callings.

Chapter 4

Our Other Responsibilities In Life

If you promise not to laugh, I'll share with you a game I sometimes played during long train delays as I commuted to and from
New York City. This is not a recommendation that you play the game
since all it did was frustrate me. I called it "Trying to find an hour
to fish."

The materials required were simple; all I needed was a pen and
paper. The purpose of the game was to see whether I could find one
hour each week to go fishing; a reasonable hour that is—not 2 a.m.

I started with an unchanging fact of life; there are 168 hours in
every week, no more and no less. My thinking was; "There must be
an hour somewhere in that time for me to go fishing, just one little
hour." So that is what I looked for. The plan was to write down
things which took time; sleep, work, church, the family, and eating.
After adding this time, what was left would be time I could use for
one hour of fishing. The first try:

Item	*Hours*	
Sleep	52½	(7½ hours per day)
Work	60	(including commuting)
Church Work	27	
Eating	10½	
Personal	10½	(½ jogging, ¼ scriptures, ¾ personal care)
Family	16	
Wife	10	
House	5	
Genealogy	2	
Journal	1½	
	195	total hours per week

47

The obvious problem with this great plan was that on our planet there are only 168 hours in each week, not 195! I therefore had two choices. I could move to a different planet—one with a 195-hour week—or I could reduce my planned hours to a total equal to no more than 168 per week. The easier option has been the second one, so far, but not by much.

If train delays were particularly long, I had time to refine my weekly plan. I attempted to reduce my planned hours to 168 and still include one hour for fishing. What I usually ended up with was total frustration, as you can see:

Item	Hours	
Sleep	48	(can't function with less)
Work	60	(can't change this)
Church Work	27	(still not doing all I should)
Eating	10½	(already eating fast)
Personal	10½	(can't cut back more here)
Family	6	(Sunday afternoon & Monday evening)
Wife	3	(Friday date)
House	3	(Saturday yard & garden)
	168	total hours per week

Although this schedule did fit into a 168-hour week, it was certainly not ideal. It put my relationship with my wife on a shelf, except for Friday evening. It provided practically no time for the children to do things with dad, eliminated such essentials as genealogy and writing in my journal, and provided no time for temple work, fellowshipping of friends and neighbors, going out with the missionaries or just relaxing for an hour of fishing. I used to think: "There has to be a more acceptable answer than this."

The question of how to fit everything we have to do, and want to do, into our busy lives can be a major source of frustration and discouragement in today's hectic world. Church members, especially those in leadership positions, are most affected by these challenges due to additional responsibilities which activity in the Church requires. We will now consider several ideas on how to deal with these challenges.

We Just Can't Do Everything

First, we must realize that we can't do everything there is to be done in this life. No matter how much we want to, or wish we could, we can't climb every mountain, ford every stream, or follow every rainbow. It is not physically possible. Furthermore, each time we do climb a certain mountain or follow a particular rainbow, we give up the option of doing something else with that piece of our lives. That time is gone. It may have been well spent with family, church, or business, but the time is gone—used up. And there are so many interesting things to do with our time that to pick and choose becomes a challenge. Yet that is what we have to do. We just can't do everything!

I don't think I began to understand this concept until after I got married. Outdoor activities had been my whole life until then. I had enjoyed them so much that I gave up sleep, missed meals, and forsook the comforts of home to do them. Almost every Saturday was dedicated to some outdoor sport.

After we were married, my wife and I settled into a small apartment on North Canyon Road in Provo, Utah. I started my last year of undergraduate studies at Brigham Young University, and my wife, Cari, started teaching at an elementary school. Then Saturday came, and in my simple, uncomplicated life I faced a major dilemma. I desired to go trout fishing with the guys on Saturday, yet I also wanted to do the activities which my wife had hoped to do with me. I could not do both. There were a number of compromises each of us could have made, but the point is that I could not do both the things I wanted to do, and the things my wife wanted me to do. I had to choose between the two interesting possibilities.

Reduce the Hours We Spend on Church Work

A basic idea on how to handle our important non-church responsibilities better is to reduce the hours we spend each week on church work by being more efficient.

This was my case as I tried to plan my time better as a bishop. It became clear that I was spending more time on church work than I was in any other area of responsibility. Church work was occupying more than four times more hours per week than was my family, and nine times more than was my wife. Yet I was still saying to myself that those twenty-seven hours of church work per week were not enough to get it all done. It is obvious that I had not yet internalized Bishop Wendell Bunker's observation that it is impossible to do all the work ourselves (see page 41). We are supposed to delegate!

With this in mind, let us consider the second idea for better handling other responsibilities in our lives. As just mentioned, the second idea is to reduce the hours we spend in church work through being more efficient. There are at least five ways to accomplish this. Since several of these methods have already been discussed, they will only be mentioned again here. The fourth and fifth ideas will be more fully developed.

1. Do "1" priorities (see page 35)
2. Delegate (see pages 38-46)
3. Use small pieces of time wisely (see page 36)
4. Streamline meetings
5. Know when to say "no"

Streamline Meetings

The fourth suggestion, streamline meetings, can save an enormous amount of time. A quick look at positions such as bishop and branch president, relief society president, stake president and others reveals that, except for preparing talks, almost all they do is hold meetings. An interview is a meeting, as is a counseling session, a planning session or a leadership gathering of any kind. In fact, any time two people meet together it can be considered a meeting.

Business executives usually spend seventy to ninety percent of their work time in meetings. Church leaders tend to spend at least that much of their church time in meetings. Because of this, the more we can learn how to make our meetings more effective, more productive—and shorter—the more we will accomplish in less time.

To streamline meetings there are a number of good ideas which both effective church and business leaders use. The use of *an agenda* is an effective idea; a brief outline of what should happen during the meeting. An agenda reminds everyone what is to be discussed, and in what order.

I have, however, been in situations where an agenda ran the meeting. Only items on the agenda would be discussed. This is too rigid. Such practices tend to cause people to lose sight of why they are there which is to effectively deal with important issues. Agendas do not run meetings—leaders do.

In order for agendas to be most effective, the executive secretary or secretary should prepare the agenda by reviewing minutes of the previous meeting. Follow-up items and topics needing additional discussion should be on the up-coming meeting's agenda. Additionally, the agenda should provide time for reports from key people, organizations, or committees. These steps alone are enough to bring more organized efficiency to most church meetings.

When an agenda is used, flexibility can be maintained if the person presiding remembers to spend the most time on "1" rated items, and not "3"s. For example, if the next item on the agenda calls for a report on a topic which needs only brief discussion, the person conducting might say, "Brother Smith, would you please give us a two-minute update on plans to repaint the cultural hall?" By saying ". . . a two-minute report . . ." the leader is not being rude. He is adding structure and discipline to the meeting. By using agendas, coupled with this leadership direction, significant improvement in effectiveness can be obtained and the total amount of time spent in meetings reduced.

Before moving to the next idea on how to streamline meetings, let's consider the following question: Should an agenda be used in meetings such as counseling sessions and interviews? Our first impression might be to answer No; that agendas would detract from the spontaneity and warmth which are important to such meetings. On closer examination, however, we may change our minds.

Returning to the definition of what is an agenda, we see that it is a brief outline of what should happen during a meeting. You might say, "All right, by that definition an agenda could be used in a counseling or interview session. But wouldn't it be a waste of time to list the obvious?" The answer is the key to success or failure in many counseling and interview situations. It is true that what you would like to have happen in meetings is often obvious: You want the person to accept a calling, change their behavior in some way, or successfully complete a worthiness interview with you. Not so obvious are the systematic steps you must go through to help get the person to that desired goal. An agenda can make it easier to follow those steps.

The type of agenda, or outline, used in a counseling or interview session is somewhat different from that used in a bishopric, primary presidency, or high council meeting, but the principle of having given forethought to your upcoming meeting by identifying a preferred sequence of events or steps which should take place, is a key to the eventual success of that meeting. In Section Two we will discuss in detail the area of counseling and interviewing. Methods of using an outline or agenda to help successfully complete counseling or interview meetings will be fully explained. For now, just remember that using an agenda is an excellent way to streamline meetings and make them more effective.

Another idea on how to streamline meetings is: *do much more deciding and much less discussing.* The principle here is quite simple: People should come to meetings prepared to make recommendations and decisions. That requires that they do brainstorming, analysis, planning, and preparation ahead of time. This suggestion alone could cut the time spent in most meetings in half and make them much more productive.

The following example shows what should happen in decision-oriented meetings. The person conducting and using an agenda—will ask for a report on a particular person, topic, or program. If the counselor or other responsible person answers by saying that everything is progressing well, he should then be prepared to briefly provide supporting information so that other people in the meeting can understand what is meant by "everything progressing well." If things are not going well the responsible person should give a three-part answer. First, a brief explanation of why things are not going well. Second, a recommendation of specific action plans to improve the situation. And third, a realistic timetable for implementing action plans with specific follow-up dates.

In order to provide a complete answer, forethought and preparation are necessary on the part of the counselor or other responsible person. Where prior preparation is not done, time must be spent during the meeting to discuss what the problem is and what should be done about it. The only other option is for the person conducting the meeting to ask that the topic be fully prepared for review later.

Start and stop on time. This is the next idea on how to streamline meetings. Like the first two ideas, this third one is an easy way to lengthen our stride—by saving time.

The person who conducts the meeting should be seated, ready to begin, five minutes ahead of starting time. That five minutes can be put to good use in reviewing the agenda. At the appointed hour the meeting should start, regardless of how many are in attendance. By following this practice consistently, coupled with a few tactfully chosen comments on punctuality prior to closing the meeting, a leader can teach members to be on time. This method really works, and it clearly can help streamline meetings.

To start meetings such as interviews and counseling sessions on time, the secret is to have your secretary telephone to remind the person or persons a day in advance. They can say something like, "This is Brother Diaz calling for President Mendez to remind you of your meeting with him at 7:30 tomorrow evening. Please be at the church before that time." This system can save bishops and presidents several hours each week.

To stop on time is essential in order to streamline meetings and be more efficient. This refers to both general and leadership meetings. Proper planning and proper control during the meeting by the person who conducts can accomplish this goal. For proper planning be sure all those who will participate know, in advance, how much time they are to take. Proper planning also means that you should not try to pack more into a meeting than can comfortably fit. Another suggestion is to always review the agenda with all who will participate such as sacrament meeting or stake conference speakers. A good time to do this final review is during the prayer meeting.

Proper control during meetings—the second part of how to end meetings on time—means that the person who conducts must remain in charge. If a discussion on one topic is taking too much time in a leadership meeting, the person conducting must step in and reassume control. This can be done by making a decision on the issue, asking someone to prepare a concise presentation with a recommendation on the topic for the next meeting, or by forcing the issue to conclusion more rapidly at the present meeting. During sacrament meetings it may be necessary, on occasion, for the person conducting to hand long-winded speakers a note which says: "Your time is up. Please stop now." In summary, starting and stopping meetings on time saves time.

Other Helpful Ideas: The next idea on how to streamline meetings a series of helpful hints. First, *always keep minutes* of leadership and presidency meetings, and reread the minutes at the start of the next meeting. Second, *review the mail ahead of time.* In this way you will be prepared to comment as appropriate on important items. Third, *only invite people to meetings if they must attend.* This will streamline the discussion and decision-making process. Fourth, *use the telephone* if you can instead of holding a meeting. Time and money saved in travel is well worth the telephone expense. Fifth, *use a calendar.* Your agenda for presidency, bishopric, and high council meetings should always call for a brief review of the calendar. Rapidly cover at least the next four to six weeks. A lot of time is saved when everyone is informed as to what activities are planned, and when. Otherwise communications break down and everyone involved wastes time.

In summary, we have discussed a number of ways to streamline meetings including use of an agenda, more deciding and less discussing, starting and stopping on time, and several other ideas. These suggestions can help reduce the number of hours we spend in church meetings without reducing our effectiveness. In fact, by using these ideas, we will be more successful in our church work with more time to spend on our other important responsibilities in life such as family, community . . . even an occasional hour for fishing!

Know When to Say "No"

The final suggestion for reducing the number of hours we spend each week on church work is to know when to say "No" to requests for our time.

There are people who feel it is disloyal—even sinful—to ever say "No" to requests for our time for church service. Effective leaders, however, have learned that there are times when it is better to say "No" to such requests. A "No" may be better for the leaders. It may be better for others, and often it is best for both parties. Let's look at why this is the case.

Our General Authorities give us clear examples of how highly effective church leaders use this principle. They are continually asked to perform marriages, speak at ward, stake, and regional firesides, give blessings, and counsel with troubled members. Directives from church headquarters continue to ask members not to make such requests of these brethren. Reasons why General Authorities say "No" to most of these requests are the same reasons bishops, stake presidents, Relief Society presidents, and many other church leaders should sometimes say "No" to requests for their time.

What are these reasons? There are two, primarily. First, the General Authorities do not have time to handle all the needs of a church membership of over five million. Second, since they understand the principles of responsibility and accountability they respect the callings other members have in the wards and stakes of Zion. Nor is there any reason why these concepts should not apply to a bishop or branch president working with his several hundred members, a Relief Society president with her 100 or 150 sisters, or to a stake leader. The principles are the same: leaders who try to do everything themselves will be less successful in getting the work done and in training other people.

Let's look at specific areas where a leader might say "No" to requests for his time. *Counseling* is one. First, except for moral matters, bishops should say "No" to the majority of counseling requests they receive. They should delegate this counseling to priesthood leaders, home teachers, or other worthy, capable members. A typical situation; an elder is having financial trouble and comes to the bishop for help in preparing a budget. The bishop, or the executive secretary, should tactfully turn the matter over to the elders quorum president. (If the elder had wanted to talk about financial assistance then the bishop would have had to handle it himself.) The elders president might then assign a quorum member with a good financial background to accompany the home teacher to a meeting with the financially struggling elder. After reviewing short-term financial obligations, and assisting the elder to set up a family budget, they would report their activities to the elder's quorum president. Further assistance could be initiated as needed, and the bishop kept informed.

Another example of where church leaders should say "No" is with members who make no effort to accept counsel and advice already given. I had to learn this concept the hard way. When I was a bishop there were people who came back to me for counsel regarding the same problem time and time again. In some cases I spent forty, fifty, or more hours with the same individuals. After all that time and effort they had not changed one bit. It is hard, but the very best thing to say to such people, after the first couple of sessions, is, "You and I both know the problem and the solution. Until you start making an effort to do what we have agreed to, I see no point in meeting again. Don't you agree?" They must accept the responsibility to make an effort to change. You can't do that for them no matter how much time you spend.

There are other times when bishops or stake presidents might say "No" to requests for their time, such as when asked to give blessings for the sick. Home teachers should enjoy the blessings which come from exercising their priesthood. Giving talks, driving youth to various activities, preparing for and cleaning up after church social events are other areas where effective leaders learn to say "No." They delegate such assignments to others, which enables them to spend more time on their other important responsibilities.

This concludes our review of ways to reduce hours spent on church work while being even more successful, and yet able to spend more time with our families, our friends, and in other important activities. A major portion of this chapter has been devoted to this topic since so many church leaders find, as I found with my 27 hours of church work per week, that they are spending more time on church callings than on any other aspect of their lives except for work and sleep.

Besides realizing we just can't do everything there is to do in life, and reducing the time we spend on church work, there are other ways to more successfully handle our important non-church responsibilities.

Do More Together As a Family

In discussing major non-church responsibilities we have, the family holds a paramount position. Members of the LDS Church often hear the statement, first made by former church president David O. McKay: "No other success in life can compensate for failure in the home." As active church leaders there are a number of things we can do to insure this success in the home. In order to better understand how to use time wisely, the following are examples of how to effectively do more as a family.

Traveling to and from church meetings is an excellent time to spend with family members. Whether you live close enough to the church building to walk to your meetings, or far enough that you must drive, take one of your children with you each time you go. Have the child or teenager take homework, a good book, their personal journal, or chalk, coloring book and crayons. In this way, they can be occupied during your meetings while waiting for you in the foyer (not in your meeting.) You can have marvelous one-to-one parent-and-child times visiting together as you go to and from meetings. Also, instead of your children saying: "Dad/Mom, do you have to go to another meeting?" They will say, "Dad/Mom, is it my turn to go to the meeting?" The difference in their attitude, and in your relationship with them, can be significant. For couples without children at home, this can be a way for the two of you to spend additional time together.

A second example of how successful church leaders can do more together with their families is related to your professional work: *Have one of your children or your spouse go with you to work.* Now before you say, "That's impossible, my boss would fire me" let me explain. I live in northern New Jersey and work in New York City. I commute by train and subway to and from work every day. From time to time I invite one of my older children or my wife to travel with me to Manhattan. The one and a quarter hour commute each way gives us an enjoyable time together. Their day is then spent at the library or museums.

In less formal work settings, it may be possible for a child to spend time in your place of work. A construction contractor friend of mine enjoys having his seven-year-old son spend an occasional morning with him at the site of a home they are building. Regardless of the situation, with a little ingenuity probably most of us can think of ways to spend time with a family member during our professional work day. Results are certainly worth the effort.

Another way that we can do more together with our families is by asking ourselves the question, *"Can I do this with a member of my family?"* If the answer is "Yes" then do it. For example, if you like to jog, jog with family members. If you run too fast have them ride along on bicycles. (That will humble you in a hurry!) If you plan to work on the yard, have the family work with you. One caution: The purpose here is to be successful with non-church responsibilities by doing more together as a family. To enjoy each other's company is part of the success. If you act like a taskmaster, barking orders to the kids, no one will enjoy it. Relax. Say to yourself, "Today I need to work in the yard. I will invite the family to be with me, not just to work, but to enjoy being together."

If you have laundry or ironing to do, dishes to wash, family budgets to plan, vacations to decide on, gardening to do, or just an hour available to go fishing, do it with a family member, not alone. You will be fulfilling important non-church responsibilities in the best possible way: together as a family.

Limit, If Not Eliminate, the Television

The last idea in this chapter concerns limiting, if not eliminating, television from our lives. We have already talked about three concepts: the impossibility of doing everything (there is to do) in life, the importance of leaders reducing time spent on church work, and the wisdom of doing more together as families. This last idea—to eliminate the TV—may not be popular with a lot of people, but I have become convinced that this can be a major factor in determining our success in both church and important non-church responsibilities.

If we go back to the beginning of this chapter to look again at my frustrating attempts to plan a 168 hour week, we are reminded how difficult it is to plan and do everything we need to. Even my 195 hour extraterrestrial week did not include television time, so where do we fit television? The answer becomes only too obvious: We fit telelvision into our lives by eliminating other things. What things? Well, we can't reduce sleep much, nor work, nor eating time, nor personal care. What is left is church work, the children, our spouse, and the house and yard. This is where television hurts us. We spend time glued to the tube instead of spending that time with the famly, our church work, or in other worthwhile pursuits. Some people think that to watch television with other family members constitutes time spent together. Wrong! If you need convincing, just try to carry on an intelligent conversation with one of your children who is watching TV. It's about as satisfying as talking to a tree trunk on a cold winter day would be. Watching television just does not qualify as time spent with the family.

Our family's regard for television was probably typical of the way many LDS families regard it. Our children watched some TV after school, and one or two programs on weeknights. Saturday seemed to be a non-stop television day, starting with cartoons in the early morning, until the late-night movie. (I never ceased to be amazed at how difficult it was for our children to get out of bed during the school week, yet how easy it was for them to get up at the crack of dawn on Saturday.) I must admit that their dad liked to spend several hours watching sports on Saturday afternoons, and it was a challenge to keep TV off on Sundays.

Television used a tremendous amount of our time, but my wife and I were even more concerned with attitudes and effects television caused in our children. My wife, Cari, used to say that she could tell if the children had been watching TV by their attitudes. The way they spoke and acted toward one another, and their reaction to being asked to do anything from coming to dinner, to homework, to help-ing around the house, to assisting with the smaller children was clearly negative and belligerent when TV had been on. In summary, it was a constant battle of who was influencing our home; the tube or the parents.

Then, over a year ago, something wonderful happened—in a puff of smoke and sparks the television stopped working. It went completely dead. Those next few weeks were extremely interesting, to say the least, since we decided not to fix or replace the TV. At first family members seemed lost, unable to decide what to do with their new-found time. And of course the children constantly reminded each other, and us, of which special programs they were missing.

Over those next weeks Cari and I started to see other interesting consequences. There was less arguing and bickering. Good books started to be read and enjoyed. Evenings other than Monday night began to seem like family home evening as we often played games together. (My wife had wisely suggested we purchase a number of fun games for both Christmas and the children's birthdays.)

Today, a year later, we still do not have a TV that works. During that year we have undoubtedly missed some fine and educational television programs. But we have also kept all the violence, the constant emphasis on sex, and the overall vice-like grip the television held over our children out of our home. During that year we have thoroughly enjoyed much more quality time together as a family with more peace, love, and kindness shown toward one another. The quality of life has been noticeably better.

The premise of Chapter five was that to be really successful as a church leader also requires that we be successful with our other important duties. We saw that this can be accomplished by carefully choosing where to spend our time, becoming as efficient as possible with our church work, doing more together as a family, knowing when to say "No" to additional requests for our time, and by limiting, if not eliminating, television.

Section II
Succeeding In Four Key Areas

Introduction

This section covers four important areas which church members should understand and practice. The focus and examples are directed more toward "how to" rather than merely "what" is important in order to be a successful leader.

The ideas discussed in this section also have broader application than for just a select few church callings such as bishop or relief society president. The explanations and examples given here are directed at priesthood, auxiliary, and stake/district leaders, as well as to visiting and home teachers.

Another primary goal of this section is to further prepare recent converts and less experienced members to be able to more quickly and successfully step into a wide range of church positions.

Chapter 5

Selecting People To Serve

What one thing do bishoprics and branch presidencies do in their meetings more than anything else? It may surprise some people to find out that in the vast majority of cases the answer to this question is: they spend most of their time selecting people to serve.

I served in bishoprics for over ten years. For the last few years, I have worked in both stake and regional positions. During that time, staffing was the one activity which took up the major portion of my time, and the time of those with whom I served. As effective leaders, we need to do an increasingly competent job of considering people for church positions, making those callings, and supporting the people we call so that they also will experience the joys of success. Through this process we will have more time to spend on other important activities. That's what we should do. Now let's look at specific ways to accomplish these goals.

Things to Consider

Two Reasons for Callings.

We have already discussed, in section one, that people are called to church positions for two reasons; one, to do the Lord's work, and two, for their own growth and further development. Let's look at these reasons more closely.

Most stakes, wards, and branches do not have an overabundance of talented leaders available to fill all positions. Most unit leaders struggle to find members able to fill the positions and successfully do work required in branches, wards, and stakes. For this reason, there may be a tendency to concentrate on getting someone to fill the position with less thought to the individual's own growth and development. These challenges can also lead to leaving people in positions for long periods, or for giving one person two or more church jobs at the same time. All this to accomplish one reason why people are called to positions; that of doing the work.

We do not want to fault leaders who have used this approach. In the majority of cases, such callings were made after sincere prayer and affirmation by the Spirit directing these leaders to make those callings. Furthermore, great blessings have come to members as they accept those callings and try to serve to the best of their ability.

The important principle for church leaders is that they continue to be careful as they select people to serve so that the welfare and growth of the individual is fully considered. This is especially true regarding new converts and recently reactivated members. Experience has shown repeatedly that it is unwise to rush recently baptized or reactivated members into major church responsibilities. When tempted to give such callings to these members leaders must objectively ask themselves, "What is best for this member to insure continued growth and development in the gospel?" If, after study and prayer a leader is still not sure, wait a little before issuing the call. It helps to remember there will always be positions to fill. What we are really interested in is people.

Strengths and Weaknesses

The importance of considering our own strengths and weaknesses, and those of other people with whom we serve, was discussed in some detail at the beginning of this book with its significance related to doing pre-work when beginning church callings. Please review those pages since the same principles apply when selecting people to serve.

It makes excellent sense to put people in positions which they enjoy, or where they have ability. Selecting members to serve in callings which require skills, talents, and interests they do not possess is risky. The probability of failure is greater when we do not match people and jobs carefully. In such mismatched cases we should be prayerfully aware of these increased risks, and try to insure that every effort is made to help these people succeed.

Consider the Big Picture

Several weeks ago I was traveling in Europe on business. International airport newsstands always attract me, especially if I can find

Swiss white chocolate (for the children, of course). After sampling the chocolate to make sure it was the kind my family liked, I browsed through the large selection of books and magazines. A booklet of crossword puzzles made in England caught my eye. I bought it.

Later, I was on an airplane feeling proud of myself, having finished my third crossword puzzle. (A secret I use is to do the ones marked "for beginners." It helps my ego.) Feeling confident, I skipped several pages to what were called "hard to do" puzzles. They weren't kidding. These seemed impossible.

One puzzle in particular confounded me. There were no numbers in the boxes. Instead, next to each clue it told how many letters the correct answer had. For example, there were twenty-one questions with a different five-letter word for each answer. Nine answers were made up of six-letter words, and so on. That meant that there were twenty-one sets of five-square boxes and nine sets of six-square boxes on the puzzle, and I had no way of knowing which correct five or six letter word went into which set of boxes.

It took what seemed like hours before I figured out where the first four words went. They were "puzzle," "zero," "error," and "caper," arranged as shown in Illustration 1.

(Ill. 1)

In order for me to complete that difficult puzzle it was important that I kept in mind the big picture. There was a temptation to write down the first two answers I knew, and which seemed to fit on the puzzle, such as "zero" and "caper" as shown in Illustration 2.

(Ill. 2)

Although "zero" and "caper" fit into the boxes, "caper" was in the wrong position. It would have caused problems had I continued to try to fill in the other boxes without moving the word "caper" to its proper position.

This example of the crossword puzzle reminded me of challenges faced by church leaders trying to fill positions in branches/wards and districts/stakes. Too often we look at one position at a time, rather than needs and strengths in the whole organization. This is short-sighted and can cause problems in selecting the right people to fill various positions.

A better approach is to look at the whole organization at the same time. By doing this, we simultaneously look at all positions and all members. The resulting big picture view can significantly improve our planning and selection of people.

In considering how to do this "whole puzzle" selection, a classic example is that of a bishop or branch president working on the staffing needs of his church unit, or quorum and Relief Society presidencies planning home and visiting teaching callings. In my experience I found that at least once a year, usually during summer months, it was necessary to make a number of major staffing changes in my ward as families moved in and out of the area.

My executive secretary would prepare several large charts with approximately seventy ward positions listed in large block letters. He would hang those charts in the bishop's office. Additionally, he listed all adult ward members on other large charts and also hung them in the bishop's office. (We found it easier to put the men and women on separate charts.)

After fasting and praying for guidance and insight we, as a bishopric, would meet together. Our first activity was to put certain key information next to each person's name which would help as we matched people and positions. Such items as current position(s), length of service in present calling(s), current level of success in position(s) held (rated 1 through 5), whether spouse had a major ward job, and any other special considerations such as "pregnant," "moving in 3 months," or "talented organist" were also listed. Illustration 3 shows how this "people chart" would look. You can add other items you consider of major importance. (*Names used here are fictitious.)

PEOPLE CHART

Name*	Position(s)	Length	Service Success	Major Spouse Calling	Other
Elizabeth Andersen	RS President	3½	1	yes	pregnant—release?
Sally Baker	Sunday Sch. Teach.	½	4	no	not enjoying call
Susan Brown	Primary 1st Couns.	2	2	yes	-
Linda Carter	YW Secretary	½	3	no	talented w/piano
Louise Elmer	None	-	-	no	possibly teach
Mary Hill	RS Spirit. Liv.	1½	1		-
	Den Mother	½	2		
Erma Johnson	None	-	-	no	-
Martha Jackson	Prim. Librarian	2	1		
	Activities Comm.	1	3	yes	moving in 1 month

(Ill. 3)

Once the "people chart" was filled out, as shown in Illustration 3, we were in a better position to consider actual staffing of the ward. This was an easy way to keep in our minds available people and their situations. It also showed positions we needed to fill. Further, it helped us keep track of what we had already planned as we went through the process of making major changes in the ward.

Before going on to the next topic on "things to consider," there may be an understandable concern generated by the previous example. People might ask, "What about letting leaders in your ward recommend their own people? It looks as if you organized the whole ward instead of letting leaders of each auxiliary and quorum do their own prayerful selection and then give you their recommendations." That is an excellent question, and it brings up an important issue.

The question is, how do people like bishops and branch presidents maintain control of the calling of members to church positions, yet give leaders who report to these bishops/branch presidents the ability to choose their own people? An example of this problem might help us.

A bishop/branch president tells his primary president to fast and pray about who she would like called to teach a particular primary class. Feeling the importance of the calling, the Primary president considers the best possible candidates, and comes up with the following people: The Relief Society president, the spiritual living leader, and the young women's Mia Maid advisor, all of whom she feels—and correctly so—would be excellent Primary teachers. She then submits the three names to the bishop/branch president.

The bishop/branch president now has a problem. He recognizes that any one of these three talented sisters would be an excellent Primary teacher, but each is already in a responsible position, doing a fine job. To release one of them and call her to the Primary position would only open her previous church job and require that it be filled. This scenario could continue indefinitely, like a giant game of musical chairs, causing endless staffing problems and precluding almost all chances of members staying in their church callings long enough to be effective.

On the other hand, if the bishop/branch president does not select one of the three sisters nominated by the Primary president he will be implying that he does not agree with her recommendations. This also has implications regarding the inspiration of the Primary president's choices. Is she more or less inspired than the bishop/branch president? This problem becomes avoidable if handled as suggested in this chapter.

To explain how to handle this situation, let's go back to the initial question, which was, "Do we let the leaders in a ward recommend their own people?" The answer is, YES! You most certainly do let them recommend the members they feel should be in their organization's positions. But—and this is just as important—you help by giving clear initial directions as to which ward members can, and which cannot, be considered for the position. In the example of the Primary president, you might provide her with a list of twenty or thirty possible candidates for the teaching position she has open. With this initial direction, your auxiliary and priesthood leaders will be able to prayerfully consider candidates for their organization without the frustration and uncertainty of not knowing whether any of those they recommend can be moved from present positions into the callings in question.

By managing the selection of members as just explained, and with a continuing view of the overall "whole puzzle," church leaders will be much more successful in staffing their church units.

Other Things to Consider

There are other important considerations for church leaders when they are selecting people to serve. One of the most practical ways to make sure each factor is taken into account is by making a check-list which you can use repeatedly. Key items you should consider, besides those already discussed, are listed here. A good way to consider these points is with a *pre-interview meeting* with the candidate during which no specific calling is mentioned.

1. *Needs of the job.* Develop a short description of what should be accomplished in the job. Give a copy of this description to the person called to the position. It will help them to know what you expect, and what you consider important.

2. *Candidate's time.* It is important to know how much time a church calling will take, and when it needs to be done. Make sure that the candidate you select will be available during those times. Otherwise your candidate cannot succeed.

3. *Candidate's work.* Closely related to the candidate's time is their work. Some professions require late evening work, or travel out of town on a regular basis. Such schedules may produce obstacles to effectively doing certain church jobs, and must be considered during the selection process.

4. *Candidate's family.* Probably no other factor influences someone more than family. This is particularly true in church callings. A supporting spouse provides encouragement, love, and the sustaining influence necessary for us to succeed. When this support is not present success becomes much more difficult. With this in mind, attention should be given to the spouse of the member being considered for a church position. It is important to consider whether his/her attitudes will undermine the chances for success of your candidate.

Another very important consideration regarding the family is the number of children still at home and their ages. No hard and fast rules can be made regarding when it would be appropriate to call someone to a position, and when it would not because of the number and ages of the children. Study each situation carefully and prayerfully before making any decision. When confronted with such challenging situations it will help to remember that the welfare of the family must always be carefully considered.

5. *Candidate's worthiness.* As a rule, we should call only worthy members to fill church jobs. That directive is a wise one to follow. It will help strengthen both members and church units. It must, however, be remembered that none of us are perfect. We all have areas where we can improve, and change—another meaning of the word "repent." Be sure that the basic commandments are being kept, and that the individual is trying to comply with the laws of the gospel. Under such circumstances the church calling will help the member grow.

6. *Candidate's level of activity.* What about calling inactive and less active members to church positions? We have all heard stories about the inactive person who responded beautifully, became totally active, and went on to be a stalwart rock of faithfulness.

Such stories are nice to hear. What we do not hear much about are situations where less active members do not work out very well in major church callings, where neither the less active member nor the church assignment are helped by such a calling. Unfortunately, this is often the case when inactive members are given major church jobs.

The moral is a simple one: be very prayerful and cautious when giving less active members major church callings. A wiser approach is to give them one of the less demanding callings available. Let them cut their teeth on that for a year or two before giving them added responsibilities. This is in the member's best interest and in the best interest of your church unit.

Choosing the Right Person

The process of how to pick the right person for a church calling has become a well-known procedure in the LDS Church thanks to modern revelation. Let's briefly review these principles and the steps one takes in order to succeed in choosing the right person for a church job.

What you need to do as you choose someone is to make a good decision as to who the person should be. So the question really is: "How do you make a good decision?" Oliver Cowdery faced this same question as he tried to translate original Book of Mormon characters. Oliver thought all he had to do was ask the Lord what was the correct translation, and the answer would be given to him. But the Lord told Oliver, as recorded in D&C 9:7-9, that it was not enough just to ask; that Oliver must study it out in his mind, meaning to ponder the matter. He was told to then make a decision—based on careful consideration. That decision was what Oliver was to pray about to the Lord in order to find out whether it was correct or incorrect. If Oliver's decision was correct, he was told that he would feel good about it. If his decision was incorrect, he would be troubled, undecided, and not able to focus on a clear answer.

This specific direction given to Oliver Cowdery on how to make good decisions, and receive confirmation by the Lord about them, should be applied by each of us as we select people to serve. Consideration should be given to each item we discussed under the heading "Things to Consider." Once we have studied these thoroughly, we will be in a position to make correct decisions and to take them to Heavenly Father in prayer for confirmation.

Now that we have discussed a number of important things leaders should consider when choosing the right person for a specific job, we are ready to talk about actually making the calling. Let's look at the specifics.

Chapter 6

How To Make Callings

When the issuing of a church call to a member is properly done, it can be an inspiring and motivating experience for all those who are involved. During such times, the Spirit of God can be unmistakably felt like a fire burning within us, as the great LDS hymn by William W. Phelps so eloquently suggests. It can be one of those prayed—for occasions when inspiration freely flows. When church callings are thus extended to the members, the chances for success by both the issuer and the receiver of the call are measurably increased.

Who To Be Present?

An important part of properly making a church calling is to determine who should be present as the call is extended to the candidate. As a rule, when the actual calling is made, only two people should be present: the issuer and the receiver of the call. Other people should not be in attendance.

There are several reasons why only these two people should be present as the call is extended. First, the candidate might say No. If that happens, it is less embarrassing if other people are not present. There may be good, yet highly personal reasons why the candidate must decline the calling. Typical reasons are a non-supporting spouse, personal health problems, personal unworthiness, or job related problems. Often, had the bishopric/branch presidency known these facts, they would have chosen another person in the first place. Yet by going through the process of issuing the call, the candidate's problems surface. Loving help can then be given. Much of this embarrassment can also be avoided by holding pre-interview meetings. (See page 69 for details).

Another reason for having only the issuer and receiver of a calling present as the call is extended is that a candidate might express concern about his ability to work well with certain leaders in the organization to which he is being called. Such frank concern would not have been expressed, and dealt with, had other people been in the meeting as the calling was given.

The third reason for only two people to be present is that the worthiness of the candidate should again be verified and it would be highly improper to have other people present at such a time.

Once the call is issued, personal worthiness reaffirmed, and acceptance is expressed by the receiver of the call, then it is not just acceptable but highly recommended for the leader issuing the call to invite other people into the room. With major callings, where considerable time will have to be devoted each week to fulfilling the church job, the spouse should be invited into the meeting. In most other cases, you will want to invite the leader of the organization in which the candidate will be serving for a brief expression of delight at the person's accepting the calling, and the chance they will have to work together. This is usually not the time, however, to orient the person in their new church position. That should be done by appropriate leaders at a separate meeting, or series of meetings.

Getting Approval From Church Leaders, Spouse, Parents

Before you sit down with a candidate to extend a church calling, make sure that you have cleared the person's name with the appropriate leaders. Clearing the person's name is an LDS way of saying that we get approval from the appropriate church authorities.

The bishop or branch president must approve all ward/branch callings. Less understood, yet just as important, is the concept of getting approval from the spouse of the person being called. If the husband is being called to serve, his wife should be asked if she will support him in his calling. If the wife is being called, then her husband should be asked if he will support her. This should be done regardless of whether or not the spouse is a member of the LDS Church. If the spouse says No, meaning that he/she will not support his/her partner in the calling, and will actively oppose it, the member should not be called to the position. Most often, however, that will not happen. Usually the spouse will appreciate your respecting him/her enough to have asked, and will support his/her partner in the calling. That support between husband and wife is an important point to establish at the outset where a married person is involved.

If you consider calling a teenager, still living at home, to a position such as pianist, chorister, secretary, primary teacher, or some other appropriate calling, you must first get approval from the teenager's parents regardless of whether the parents are members of the church. The same principle should apply when calling youth to various quorum and class presidency positions. Get their parents involved. Don't lose sight of the fact that all of these organizations, callings, and activities are to help support the family unit, not replace it. Church leaders should therefore make sure they help parents get as actively involved as possible.

The Setting

Sacrament meeting was going to start in three minutes as Brother Jones, second counselor in the bishopric, quickly walked down the corridor looking for Sister Larsen. He spotted her as she was about to enter the chapel, two small children at her side. Brother Jones called to her from across the foyer, "Sister Larsen, may I speak to you for a moment?" There, three feet from the busy chapel entrance, Brother Jones asked, "Would you be interested in being a Relief Society teacher? We would like to present your name in sacrament meeting today."

How many things can you identify in the previous paragraph which are incorrect? There are at least seven I can think of.

1. Three minutes before sacrament meeting is not enough time to properly extend a call to serve in a church position.

2. Brother Jones should have been seated at the front of the chapel to show, by example, the importance of reverence, especially just three minutes before sacrament meeting was to start. If leaders preach reverence, they must practice it also. If they don't preach it, they should!

3. Sister Larsen had her two small children with her, a definite potential source of distraction during the conversation.

4. As Brother Jones called to Sister Larsen from across the foyer, he was telegraphing to everyone present his interest in talking to her about something, thereby reducing the confidentiality of the issue. Again, he was not setting a good example regarding reverence.

5. A call to serve, issued three feet from a busy chapel entrance, is in poor taste. Confidentiality is almost totally eliminated, as is a warm personal touch which is what leadership style in the Church is

all about. The significance and importance of the matter is clearly reduced through such actions.

6. When calling someone to serve, it is incorrect to say, "Would you be interested in being a Relief Society teacher?" The issue is not, "Would you be interested," but rather, "The Lord has called you through the bishop/branch president to serve. Do you accept?"

7. By Brother Jones saying that he wanted to present Sister Larsen's name to the congregation "today," he meant in the meeting which was going to start in less than three minutes. No time was given Sister Larsen to think and pray about the calling, nor was there sufficient time to talk to her husband to seek his support.

From this example it is clear that the setting surrounding a church calling can make a significant difference. The setting consists of place, timing and atmosphere surrounding a church calling.

The Place

The bishop/branch president's office, the stake/district president's office, or a vacant classroom which will not be disturbed are all appropriate places to issue a calling. There are times when going to the candidate's home or having the person come to your home might be appropriate. In such cases, make very sure that other people will be in the home, but not in the area where the calling is to be extended.

The Timing

As to timing, the secret is to allow enough time: time to issue the call, time to discuss the calling with the candidate's spouse or parents, and time for the candidate to prayerfully consider their response.

Success in issuing church calls will be measurably improved by following this counsel.

The Atmosphere

Both place and timing add to, or detract from, the overall atmosphere which is present while the calling is being given. Additionally, if you as the leader are rushed, preoccupied with other matters, or for some reason are not totally relaxed and friendly, yet businesslike, your lack of interest and negative style will be immediately felt by the candidate. In order for the atmosphere to be good, it requires that you make a conscious effort in the areas just mentioned. As you do, the setting within which you call members to church positions will strengthen the significance of those callings, and help insure both their success, and yours.

What To Include In a Calling

When calling someone to serve in the Church, there are specific items which should be included as part of the calling whether you are calling someone to be a stake president, a visiting or home teacher, a priesthood leader, or a class or quorum teacher. It is amazing how often several of these items are not included. Then we wonder why people quit, why jobs are not done as we hoped they would be, and why we are spending all of our time on staffing. Let's review what these important items are.

Called of God

We believe that members are called to church positions by God, through His duly appointed representatives here on earth. This is the Church of Jesus Christ, and prophecy, revelation, and inspiration are the channels by which the Spirit of the Lord informs church leaders of the will of the Father and the Son. As mortals, we may not fully understand how this process works. Some may not even have an abiding faith that it does always work. But the reality is that it surely does function that way, and that the Lord continually directs His Church, and will not permit us as mortals to cause it to fail. He has promised us that.

Because of the foregoing explanation, and after doing our part of the decision-making process as already explained, it is totally appropriate when calling someone to serve, to say, "The Lord has called you through the bishop/branch president (or stake/district president) to serve." Then specify the position to which the person is called.

Duties and Responsibilities

After telling someone that they have been called to a particular church position by God, through His duly-appointed church leaders, the next thing to be done is to tell the person a little about the calling.

There are members who do not have a good understanding of duties and responsibilities of various church jobs. This is not surprising. A member may have served for a year or two in one church position. A call to serve in a different position would require different duties and responsibilities. It would take years to learn each church job well. We must not suppose that members will know all about their new calling. In fact, it is wise to assume that they know little about the duties of a new church job.

The job description, which was hopefully prepared as the needs of the calling were initially considered and as the selection process took place, should now be given to the newly called member. A good job description will explain the duties and responsibilities and should be as specific as possible.

Let's look at how a job description can help to clearly communicate duties and responsibilities of the calling. If you expect the member to do seven things as part of his church calling, we will represent those seven activities by making a box (labeled A.B.C.D.), as shown in illustration number 4. If the member did seven activities (shown as rectangle E.F.G.H.) but only four of the seven are on your list of seven (namely E.F.I.D.) you have a communications problem. This typical leadership problem can be easily solved by doing two things. First, provide the newly called person with a clear list of

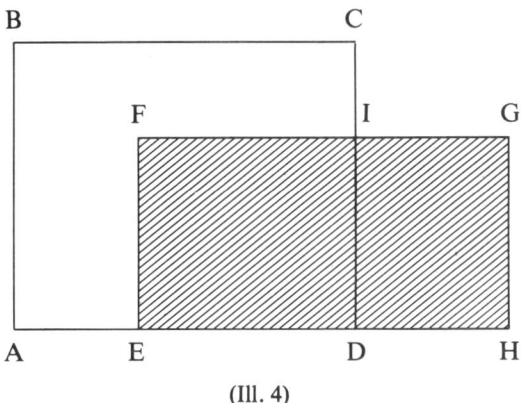

(Ill. 4)

duties and responsibilities when he receives his calling. And second, on a regular basis, sit down with the member and review how he is doing. In that way you can insure that A.B.C.D. is being done, not E.F.G.H.

Meetings to Attend

It could be argued that meetings a newly called member is to attend are part of his duties and responsibilities. I won't argue the point. What is important is that, as you call someone to a church job, you clearly let him know what meetings he is expected to attend. There will never be a better time to reinforce the importance of the member's attending appropriate meetings. If there is going to be a problem with the newly called member being able to attend the meetings you need to know now—right up front—not three months later.

Meetings to attend should include sacrament meeting, priesthood meeting for the men and Relief Society for the women, and leadership and faculty meetings at the ward/branch, stake/district, and regional level. It is also appropriate to include temple attendance at this time. It strengthens and helps us all, when we have been challenged to meet specific goals and objectives, to know clearly what is expected of us.

Reporting Relationships

The purpose of explaining all reporting relationships when issuing a call is so that the candidate will clearly understand with whom he will be working, and to whom he may turn for help. We all want to know these things. It provides a source of comfort and reassurance to hear that there are leaders out there who will take a special interest in us. It also helps define to whom the newly called member should not go for initial help. We don't want everyone in the ward going to the bishop with every question and concern. Similarly, it is not appropriate for members to go directly to general authorities with their questions, concerns, and problems. We are to follow the established lines of authority and go to our immediate leaders for help.

Called For How Long?

Recently, bishops are being called to serve for approximately 5 years, mission presidents for 3 years, missionaries for 18 months, and stake presidents for approximately 10 years. But what about Sunday School teachers and auxiliary presidency members? With certain callings there has been a generally accepted length of time to serve, which is usually explained to the person as the call is received. You should do the same thing with all other church callings.

More times than I care to count I have had the experience of calling someone to serve only to have him quit after a month, or two, or possibly six. This is extremely disruptive to the planning and staffing processes of church units. Furthermore, the organizations in which the members served, and the individual lives of people—especially children and youth—with whom the members may have been working, are also disturbed. Lack of consistency in such situations can become a major problem for unit leaders.

Later in this chapter we will discuss how to deal with people who who want to be released. The important point here, and a factor in eliminating this problem, is to specify a length of service for whatever calling you are extending. In most cases the length of service you indicate to church members should be at least one to two years— preferably two years. Take it from someone who has learned the hard way, by trial and error, it does not work to ignore or sidestep this issue. If you wish to succeed you have to take the initiative.

Asking Questions During the Calling

There are certain questions you need to ask as you call someone to serve, usually toward the end of the meeting with the candidate and before you bring anyone else into the room.

1. "Do you have any questions about what I have said so far?" Through this question you can make sure there are no major areas of concern or doubt on the part of the candidate. You can also reinforce that appropriate unit leaders who will be working with the person will help answer questions the candidate is bound to think of.

2. "Are there any reasons why you should not be called to this position; family, personal, or worthiness reasons? Please think carefully." This is a powerfully worded question, but it should be asked. Often the candidate will have concerns about problems or situations in his life which could hinder his effectiveness. These concerns should be expressed and resolved. If moral issues are alluded to which involve the candidate, then the interview should stop at that point unless you are the bishop/branch president, and should be turned over to the bishop/branch president. If concerns are mentioned on other matters, try to deal with them and help the candidate. (See chapter 8 in this section, on counseling, for specific ideas on this subject.) In many cases there will not be any problems; but make sure to ask.

3. "Do you accept the church calling as I have explained it?" It is important for the person to make a firm commitment of, "Yes, I accept," or a similar response. He should not just listen and then say, "I'll try it." If the person is not sure, do not try too hard to convince him. A famous saying is applicable here: "A person convinced against his will, remains of the same opinion still." Let the person go home and pray about that calling. Then get together to discuss it again. That extra time is well worth taking. Remember, your goal is to have

that person fill the job in question for one to two years, or more—not one or two months.

Final Remarks When Issuing a Call

Before closing the meeting, often by a prayer, there are other items you will need to mention to the newly called member.

1. When and where additional training and instruction will take place, and by whom.

2. Which handbooks the person should read and where to obtain them. (Try to provide necessary handbooks at the time of the call.)

3. When the person's name will be presented to the congregation for a sustaining vote.

4. When the person will be set apart, and who will perform the ordinance. Normally the bishopric/branch presidency or stake/district leaders will do the setting apart. (Make sure to record who set the person apart, and when. For some reason, this step is often forgotten.)

5. Whether or not the person can discuss this calling with other people. Usually, other than immediate family and those leaders with whom the person will work, no comments should be made to other people. This is especially important if a series of moves are anticipated in the church unit which will involve several people. In such situations, misunderstandings can easily arise. The best rule to follow is to say. "Please don't talk about this calling to anyone until after your name is presented to the congregation for a sustaining vote."

6. A closing statement of support for and confidence in the person is always appropriate and appreciated.

Before ending this chapter on how to make church callings, there is another important question related to this topic which is now presented.

What To Do When a Person Wants To Be Released

The key word in this statement is the word "wants." It tips you off to the basic reason for the member to decide to resign. He is having problems which are preventing him from being successful in his church calling, and which are causing him to want to be released.

Had the member said he "had" to be released, the implication would have been that he doesn't want to—but has to—resign. This happens when the member is moving out of your church unit, or when health, family, or business reasons prevent the member from continuing in his calling. The best approach in this case is to express sincere appreciation for the member's having served, regret for his not being able to continue, and total acceptance of the situation. Be understanding, not condemning.

But what about when a member does not have to be released, but wants to be? Let's discuss specific things church leaders can do under such circumstances. (In addition to what we will mention in the next few pages, both Chapters 7 and 8 in this section, which deal with interviewing and counseling, will be helpful as you face this leadership challenge.)

Find Out What Is Causing Problems

The first thing to do when a person wants to resign is to find out what is causing the problem(s). There have to be reasons why the member wants to be released; reasons at the core of the problem. In order to determine what those reasons are, the following three steps can be very helpful.

1. *Ask the person.* Members may not know why they want to quit, but by getting the person to talk about the situation, the real reasons will usually be evident.

2. *Ask other people,* especially those who work closely with the member who wants to resign. Great care must be used here since the request to resign is usually confidential, not public. The general membership should not be aware that a change will take place until the official announcement is made across the pulpit. With prudence you can, however, obtain information which will help you better understand what is causing the problem(s). Ask such questions as, "How much training and orientation has the member had?" "How long has the person been in the position?" "How difficult is the job the member has?" (Teaching 25 three-year-olds single-handedly will cause the most hearty person to want to be released!) "How much support is the member receiving from other leaders, family and friends?"

3. *Observation of the member performing* his calling will also help you gain insight into why the member is having problems.

Only after you have ideas as to why the member is not having success, and what problems are causing him to want to be released, will you be in a position to decide what to do.

Can The Situation Be Corrected?

Once you know why the member is having problems and not being successful, you have to make a difficult decision. You have to decide whether the situation can be corrected while the member remains in the church calling, or whether the person should be released. To help you make a better decision let's consider consequences of the two alternatives.

If the situation can be corrected while the member remains in the church calling, that is often the best alternative since the member will be strengthened, have a positive church experience, and the job will get done. But to correct causes which are behind the member's wanting to be released will require time and effort; not necessarily yours, but certainly someone's. It will probably require more training of the member, added support by showing the member how to do various aspects of his job better, and in some cases either an assistant should be assigned or the job restructured to ease the work load. Such efforts are well worth the time and effort and probably should have been done in the first place.

If you have trained leaders available and willing to train, teach, and show the struggling member how to do his job, try to get the member to stick with the calling for at least another few months. Even if the match-up of job and person is not ideal (and it rarely is), the hope is that the member will have positive experiences and feel better about himself and the calling before he is released. We do not want our members to go from one bad experience to another, from one failure to another. That is certainly not the way the Lord intends His Church to be run.

The second alternative is to release the member now. But before you make that decision, consider the consequences. You will probably have a member who feels bad—often guilty—that he was not able to do the job to which he was called, sustained, and set apart. And there are often feelings of "I let my leaders down." The job did not get done well and the member did not have a positive growth experience, both negative results. And what about the attitude of the member toward future church callings? Often there will be reluctance and fear about accepting new assignments.

Recognizing possible negative consequences of releasing a member who struggles and does not fulfill his job very well, a leader might be tempted to try to convince such members to stick with their calling. This thought is noble, but the idea will certainly backfire and cause the leader to lose member support and even respect unless the leader takes additional action. The leader must help the member to succeed because if the leadership situation remains unchanged the struggling member will get the same kind of help and support, or lack thereof, which had been given in the past—and that was inadequate. The answer, if it is at all possible, is to get the member to stay in the job while you and your other leaders provide the support necessary for the member to succeed.

There will be occasions when the member must be released; when you just can't have him remain in the position any longer. When that is the decision be sure to do three things:

1. Identify positive things you can honestly say about his performance. You might mention an excellent attendance record, his charts and other visual aids, or specific successes. There always are genuine and positive things to mention.

2. Call the person to another church assignment at the time of the release, if possible. You want the person to recognize that you continue to feel that he is a valuable asset and important part of your church unit.

3. Specify helps you plan for his new calling. Help him to envision a success experience. Be positive, excited about the future, and show confidence in the person. Then be absolutely sure to follow through. That will produce success.

This concludes our chapter on how to make callings in the church. We have considered who should be present during the call, getting approvals, the setting, specific things to include during the call, and how to deal with people who want to be released. Let us now turn to the subject of interviewing.

Chapter 7

Interviewing

Interviewing is such a fundamental part of so many church callings that it should be considered among the most important skills leaders must possess.

Virtually every church calling uses interviewing to some degree. Can you conceive of a General Authority, a stake president, a bishop, a Relief Society president, or a priesthood leader who does not do a lot of interviewing? Think of such activities as staff selections, counseling members, progress reviews, church courts, advancement and worthiness interviews. Add to this list home and visiting teachers who use an informal interview to review the general welfare of members to whom they are assigned. Now you have an impressive case for the importance of good interviewing skills.

Fortunately, with only modest effort, almost anyone can develop these interview skills. They can be learned by all who are willing to follow steps outlined in this chapter.

Key To Success: Be Prepared

The Boyscout motto is: Be prepared. That time-tested good counsel is applicable in every facet of our lives whether in school, on the job, with our families, in sports, or in our church assignments. In interviewing, being prepared is the most important ingredient for success.

There are four specific areas of preparedness in interviewing which, when followed, will measureably improve results. These areas will help whether you are selecting staff, counseling members, conducting a church court, holding an advancement or worthiness interview, reviewing a member's progress in an assignment (often called a PPI—personal priesthood interview), or visiting with an assigned family as a home or visiting teacher.

1. *Know facts ahead of time.* The first thing to do, when preparing to conduct an interview, is to find out as much as you can about the person, the situation, and/or the problem(s) before the interview. This first step is crucial since it forms the framework upon which the interview will be built. You can't ask intelligent questions unless you know what you need to find out, and you won't know areas to emphasize, downplay, or purposely ignore unless you have first obtained background information.

In summary, the more you know ahead of time about the person, the calling, the problem(s), expected results, or church policies on a particular issue, the more effective and successful you will be during the interview.

2. *Decide on the desired outcome.* The second important activity, when you are preparing to conduct an interview, is to decide on the desired outcome ahead of time. This may sound either obvious or unnecessary but it is a significant factor in achieving success in interviewing.

To better understand this concept, let's consider the example of an important trip by car. It is critical on such a trip to know where you want to be at the end of your journey, otherwise you probably won't arrive at your desired destination. It is only by keeping that final destination—or outcome—firmly in mind that you will make correct decisions along the route as to which direction you need to travel, and which roads you must not take.

Similarly, in interviewing, we must decide—and keep firmly in mind—the final destination—or outcome—we wish to achieve. In that way we will be able to ask the right questions, and direct the flow of the meeting to reach our final objective.

Let us consider an elders quorum president as he interviews a home teacher. The desired outcome of this meeting could be to get specific information on the status of each family for whom the home teacher is responsible, or it might be to find out why the junior companion is not being used by the home teacher, so as to change that situation. A third desired outcome could be to find out why the home teacher is not visiting his families and to decide on the best approach to use to help him fulfill his calling in the future. Each of these desired outcomes is different. Each requires different questions, and use of a different approach in order for the interview to be successful. To keep the desired outcome firmly in mind is an important step to being prepared in interviewing.

3. *Develop questions ahead of time.* For the last few years I have had the opportunity of lecturing at Brigham Young University to students in the Master of Business Administration and Organizational Behavior Programs. This has given me the chance to occasionally interview students for the multinational corporation for which I work. When doing this kind of interviewing it quickly becomes apparent that you have to be well prepared ahead of time. These students are articulate, well prepared, and generally competent interviewers. It is not sufficient to just "visit" with them for a few minutes. In order to be able to decide which students are viable candidates for a certain job, in a particular company, it is necessary to develop specific questions ahead of time which will help in the selection process.

If the job I am looking to fill is in marketing, I develop eight or ten specific questions which will show me whether the student is a good candidate for marketing. If the positions to be filled are in financial planning, or human resource management, I develop very different sets of questions.

Some people may feel that interviewing techniques in the Church are not similar to interviewing techniques in the business world. But actually they are very similar. After you identify as many facts as possible before the interview, and decide on the desired outcome of the meeting, you should develop specific questions—ahead of time— which will provide you with the information you need. In summary, don't wait until you are in the middle of an interview to try to think of what to ask, and how to say it.

4. *Develop contingencies based on possible answers.* Being prepared is the best way to stay out of trouble. It is also the best way to get out of trouble once you are in a difficult situation. Do this by considering possible answers you could get to your questions, and by developing contingency plans based on those possible answers.

Let's look at a typical example of how contingency planning works in church interviews. In the last chapter we talked about how to call members to church positions. We also said that one thing which sometimes happens is that the person receiving the church calling will say "No," meaning he will not—or can not—accept the call to serve. That can be an awkward situation for both people unless the interviewer has anticipated this possible response to the call, and has developed a contingency plan on how to handle the situation.

This kind of challenge occurs with frequency as you interview people, and with interviews of all kinds, not just those in which people are called to serve. Consider a worthiness interview, where the question of moral cleanliness is asked. In today's extremely permissive society the incidence of every kind of moral problem is on the increase. Certainly the overall frequency of moral problems is much less among church members than among the world's general population, but some members do have problems. Church leaders must therefore be prepared, and also know what to do and say at such times. This can be accomplished by anticipating such possibilities, and by developing alternate approaches ahead of time.

What should you do when the person you are interviewing for advancement in the priesthood says he is not sure he wants to accept the higher priesthood? What about the youth you says he will no longer attend seminary? What about the visiting teacher who asks one of her families how things are going, and is told that they are thinking of getting a divorce? The list could go on and on. The point becomes very clear that, as leaders, we need to be prepared for interviews we conduct. One of the ways to be prepared is to develop contingency plans of what to say and do based on possible answers to different questions.

Atmosphere

In order to be successful in interviewing church members, you have to get the people you are talking with to share their thoughts and feelings, and a portion of their lives. If you cannot get the interviewee to open up and share, your interviews will be much less effective. So how do you get people you interview to share their thoughts and personal selves?

There are several things interviewers can do. We have already discussed the importance of being well prepared. Later in this chapter we will talk about how to ask the right questions. But there is one other factor which is essential in church interviews if you are going to get members to share their very personal lives with you. That factor is the atmosphere you create during the meeting. Without it all the preparation and good questions in the world will be largely ineffective.

Warm, Caring, and With Compassion

Atmosphere is best described as the environment within which the interview takes place. For example, one person being interviewed might feel perfectly at ease, comfortable with the interviewer, and willing to share personal feelings. We could say that the atmosphere in the meeting was warm and caring with a tone of compassion and expectation of openness definitely present. In an opposite situation, the member being interviewed might feel very ill at ease, uncomfortable with the interviewer, and unwilling to share personal feelings. In such a meeting we would say the atmosphere was cold and indifferent, with less feeling of compassion evident, often due to a more rigid leadership style. From these descriptions of the atmosphere, it is easier to understand why atmosphere is such an important factor in the outcome of church interviews.

In looking at the difference in atmosphere between the two interviews just mentioned, one of the things we did not mention was the purpose, or reason for the meetings. There is a good reason why this was not mentioned, and that is to emphasize the point that the atmosphere in a meeting is a product of the interviewer's style, regardless of the purpose of the meeting. You will notice that in the more open, warm meeting words such as, "feel at ease," "comfortable with the interviewer," "willing to share," "warm," "caring," "tone of compassion," and "expectation of openness" were used to express the mood and tone established by the interviewer's style of leadership.

I have been present during particularly difficult situations, such as where a bishop's court had to interview an individual for very serious infractions, yet the presiding leader was still able to establish an environment of trust, caring, and compassion. When that kind of atmosphere is established, it is in large measure the direct result of efforts made by the leader who is conducting the meeting. It is not an accident. With that kind of warm, caring atmosphere, the leader will be much more successful in completing the interview.

Before leaving this topic of atmosphere you create, one word of caution should be given regarding the relationship which is developed with members of the opposite sex. In developing the warm, caring environment we just discussed, it is mandatory that the relationship with each member be one of total righteousness and integrity. Even the slightest hint of anything less is completely out of line. This point cannot be stated too strongly.

In order to make very sure that no one will ever misunderstand or have cause to wonder about your motives and integrity, here are two helpful suggestions.

1. First, do not meet with members of the opposite sex under potentially dangerous circumstances, such as just the two of you meeting late at night at the church, or at a home. Meet at times and places where other people are in the immediate area—not present, but nearby.

2. Second, make sure you convey the feeling that you are an official of the Church, conducting the Lord's business, and not a member of the opposite sex, as you interview members. To do this, be careful with the intent of your smiles, the level of warmth in your voice, your manners, gestures, and the interviewing questions you choose. If you realize that you would tone down or change your mannerisms and questions in any way if your spouse or a General Authority were in the room quietly observing you as you interviewed or counseled with the member, then something is very wrong. You are flirting with disaster, and must repent—meaning change at once.

The high and noble positions in the Church which require, as part of their calling, the personal interviewing of members, demand that we be righteous, that we shun the slightest semblance of evil. By so conducting ourselves we will find both joy and success in fulfilling our labors in the Church.

Asking the Right Questions

When we think about interviewing, what usually comes to mind is one person asking questions of another to obtain information. Asking and answering questions are the basic activities in an interview.

Asking questions is the way an interviewer obtains information. To ask the right ones will make a big difference in the success an interviewer has. For this reason, we will now discuss how to ask the right questions in various interviewing situations.

Before we start let's briefly analyze the three sections which make up the interview. This will help us to better understand what types of questions to ask, and when.

Starting the Interview

In beginning an interview, thank the person for meeting with you. Spend a few minutes (no more than 3-5) visiting with the member in a warm and friendly manner before you start the main questioning. This will help the person to relax. But don't overdo this initial visit. In most cases, you both know why you are meeting together, which is to conduct an interview. Spending too much time on chitchat will waste time and may increase the anxiety level for both of you.

Introductory questions might include: "How was the traffic this evening?" "Did Mary get back from camp?" "Tell me about your fishing trip." None of these are questions where the interviewee can easily answer with yes or no, and this is important. As quickly as possible you want to get the people talking, and the best way to do that is to ask them open-ended questions about themselves or their family. Do not begin these questions with the words "is" or "was" which lead straight to yes or no answers. Use words such as "Tell me" to start these introductory questions.

Main Body Of the Interview

After this introductory conversation move into the main body of the interview with a transition statement: "The main purpose of our meeting is to review your home teaching families. I have several questions to ask. Is it all right if we do that and begin with a prayer?"

Another transition statement might be: "Sister Marquez, it's a delight to visit with you. As you know the purpose of our meeting is to renew your temple recommend. Would you like to begin the interview by offering an opening prayer?" Other introductory statements might include a mention that the interview will remain confidential.

From this point you should ask the questions you have prepared or questions which have been prepared for you, such as with a temple recommend interview. Continue to ask questions until you have obtained the information you need, or until it is evident that no purpose would be served by asking additional questions. At that point offer concluding remarks and end the interview.

Ending the Interview

At the conclusion of every interview, summarize or review any action plans decided on and reinforce follow-up dates. Express your sincere appreciation for the member's having met with you. Finally, it is almost always appropriate to end with a prayer.

Determining the Truth

Before discussing specific types of questions which can be used in the main body of an interview, we need to talk about a challenging yet important topic for church leaders: determining the truth.

In the business world it is generally recognized that people often do not tell the whole truth. A totally honest person is unfortunately a rather rare commodity in today's world.

Members of The Church of Jesus Christ must recognize that members come from—and live in—the world where temptations, influences and behavior patterns influence each of us to some degree.

No one likes to discuss old skeletons in his closet about personal or family problems still unresolved. There are pressures from several sources such as: "What will the bishop/branch president think of me?" "What if my spouse finds out?" or "Will I lose my church membership?" which influence the decision about telling the whole truth. How many times do Relief Society or elders quorum presidents call on a member who is having problems only to be told that everything is OK?

The point of this discussion is that interviewing in the Church is used to obtain valid information, yet not every member is fully truthful. When that happens, the church leader is handicapped in both counseling and in making good decisions. For these reasons it is important for leaders to know how to ask questons which will help them determine the full truth.

A factor which helps church leaders in determining the truth is the spirit of discernment. This gift is given for the purpose of helping church leaders to understand reality and truth. (Section Three of this book discusses this, and other aspects of what can be called the spiritual side of church leadership.)

Recognizing that the Lord blesses and helps us when we do all that we can, let's return to the issue of how to ask the right questions in an interview. We will look at four kinds of questions. Knowing how and when to use each will help you to be more successful in interviewing.

Open-Ended Questions

An open-ended question is recognized by its being general in what it asks. When using such questions you avoid specifics. A typical open-ended question is: "Please tell me about yourself." Another example would be: "In your own words, please tell about the situation." The person is simply asked to tell you about himself or a situation. He is usually not told what to include and what to omit, how long to talk, how much detail to give, or how to organize his thoughts. Depending on your needs as the interviewer, you can always add more specifics to the questions.

There are several reasons to use open-ended questions. First, this kind of question is much less threatening than a direct question such as: "Would you please help me understand why you have not taught your class for the last three weeks?" Such a specific question might be appropriate later on but more general, open-ended questions are usually a better way to start. Another good reason to use open-ended questions is that you are not telegraphing your feelings and thoughts as you ask the question. The person being interviewed must, therefore, give you an answer without knowing what you think or know about the matter. Open-ended questions are also good because the person being interviewed usually provides you with a broad answer, often covering a lot of area and subject matter. In this way you often learn things you did not know and which would have been impossible to ask questions about earlier.

There are two other points to consider when using an open-ended question. First, try not to interrupt the person while he is talking. This is not the time to break in and ask for more details. You will have a chance to do that later. More information will be obtained if you just listen. The second important point is that while the person is talking, you try to concentrate and listen as hard as you can to what is being said. We will discuss listening in detail later. Many of your more specific and follow-up questions can be based on information you get during this time. In summary, open-ended questions are useful tools to use in interviewing, especially during the early part of the meeting.

Specific Questions

The time comes in every interview when you should get more specific. It's not usually acceptable to keep the whole meeting on a superficial level of questions and answers. That is why specific questions are important.

A specific question can be defined as a clear and concise question which goes right to the point: "Do you pay tithing?" is not too bad as specific questions go. "Do you pay a full and honest tithing?" is a far better question since it is even more specific.

Once you have spent anywhere from a few minutes to fifteen minutes on open-ended questions, you should switch to more specific questions. In order to help the member accept the transition from open-ended to specific questions, you might say, "I appreciate your sharing both personal feelings and a portion of your life with me. It is not always easy to do that. There are a few rather specific questions I would now like to ask you." Start with questions which are not too sensitive or difficult to answer. Begin with a nonthreatening specific question about something the member said earlier in the interview. By doing this you show the interviewee that you listened and were interested in what was said. From this point on you can move to more difficult or sensitive issues and questions.

Using specific questions may sound simple and straight-forward, but selecting the right words in order to zero in on issues and help the members to discuss and not side-step issues can be very challenging. Let's look at two examples to understand how this is accomplished. First, how will we get more information from a member we know is having difficult family problems? Knowing ahead of time that there are problems is a help in getting the person to answer, and not avoid the issue by saying, "Everything is fine."

Let the member being interviewed know that you are already aware that there is a problem. This is the real key in helping members to answer you fully. You must be very sure of your information before you begin or you will lose creditability. Listen to the promptings of the Spirit. Look for signs to support your strong feelings that the member was having real problems. Then begin your specific questions with a statement to that effect. You might say, "I have a feeling things are not going well for you right now. Would you help me to understand why?" It is hard for a member to evade or ignore such a specific question.

The second example of using a specific question when the member has a problem is when you are not aware that there is a problem. You might feel uneasy as the Spirit prompts you to become concerned, or you may not have been forewarned that there was a problem. These situations are more difficult to handle, but as leaders we must try to be successful. We have to walk a fine line between being an eternal optimist or an eternal pessimist.

Let me explain. It would ill-become church leaders to assume that everyone they interview has problems. It is more constructive to look for the good in people, not the bad. On the other hand, we all know that none of us is perfect; that we live in a world where serious problems periodically confront us all. Every one of us has personal challenges, and areas where we can improve. Therefore, in asking specific questions during interviews, assume that the member is trying to do his best, and that he is facing many of life's challenges quite well. However, don't stop there. Recognize that there are still difficult challenges the person will face and that there will be areas where the member can further improve. In this way, you can help interviewees recognize and feel proud about all the good things, while identifying and working to improve areas of continuing challenge.

So how do we do this in an interview? The answer is that we ask specific questions which cover the major elements of significance in our lives. The temple recommend interview is an excellent blueprint to use in accomplishing this. Certainly questions must be modified to fit the person and the situation, but the major questions are all there. Morality (for bishops to cover), supporting church leaders, word of wisdom, tithing, attitudes toward service in the Church, relationships, and the chance to fully repent are each covered. Within the guidelines established by the Church, these questions should be asked in church interviews.

It is unfortunate, but sometimes these specific questions are not asked. Have you ever been in an interview where the person simply said something like: "Are you living the gospel?" You probably thought for a moment and then said, "Yes, I think so. I am trying." To that the leader said, "Good, I thought you were." And that is the end of the interview. The leader may think that not asking specific questions is, in some way, a compliment. In fact, it is very unfair. If the person is living the gospel, it is because of real efforts on his part. To hold and conclude an interview in such a rapid, nonchalant manner will not help motivate anybody to live the gospel better which is a primary reason for holding interviews.

If the person is not living the gospel as he should, and is not telling the truth, such a curt interview will not help motivate the person to improve, or to strenghen his self image. In summary, we must carefully use specific questions in interviewing in order to be really effective and successful.

Follow-up Questions

We have finally gotten to the questions which, when properly used, can provide you with the most specific and informative answers: follow-up questions. As the name implies, these questions are used by asking a second, third, or even fourth specific question about the same topic in order to obtain more information, or to further clarify something.

The value in follow-up questions is that they help to more accurately determine the whole truth. For example, let's assume you are interviewing a teenager and begin, "Tell me how things are going with you"—an open-ended question. The youth will probably reply, "Not too bad." It would be a foolish leader who would then say, "Good, I am glad to hear you are OK," and end the interview there. "Not too bad" can mean anything—literally anything—from the youth doing well to having major and serious problems. The interviewer must not guess—or assume he knows—what is meant by such an ambiguous statement. More follow-up questions must be asked.

A good way for the interviewer to continue would be by asking a more specific question; "I know life can be a challenge, and that in today's world it can seem almost impossible sometimes to live the gospel. Please share with me some of the things which are not going too well for you right now." The teenager might say, "Well, there aren't real bad problems. You're right, though, that pressures are real strong from the kids." An answer similar to this says several things. What it does not say is that everything is just fine. By the youth saying that "there aren't real bad problems" it would seem to imply that there are some problems—less serious, maybe, in the youth's eyes—but problems. The teenager is also admitting intensive peer pressure, which again implies that problems may exist. More follow-up questions must be asked.

Follow-up questions, then, are one of the best tools an interviewer can use to get specific information, and to make sure that situations and feelings are understood to be what they really are. The use of follow-up questioning will make a noticeable improvement in the success a leader has in interviewing.

Leading Questions

Before leaving the topic of "Asking the Right Questions" a word or two should be said about the problem of leading questions. By definition, a leading question tells the person being interviewed what you, the interviewer, think, or feel, or believe to be the right answer to the question you are asking.

Some obvious leading questions are: "I don't think we should do that youth activity, what do you think?" or: "Let's certainly hope that you have not slipped. Have you kept the Word of Wisdom?"

A third obvious example of a leading question is: "Weeknights are usually bad for me to visit in your home, don't you think?" In each of these examples, the person asking the question is interjecting his own prejudices.

The problem with using leading questions in an interview is that pressure is applied on the person being interviewed to answer the question as he thinks you want him to, and not as the member might like to answer. He may answer as he thinks you would like him to, but the answer you hear may not represent what the member really feels or wishes. And the problem with this is that you are trying to find out what the member thinks and feels, and how he is living. You are not interested in the person parroting back to you what you believe; information of little help to a leader.

It is impossible to completely avoid leading questions. When you ask someone if he is living the Word of Wisdom, he knows you are interested in that topic, and that you think it is important to live that law. That cannot be avoided unless you never ask specific questions, which would not be a good interviewing technique. So be careful when you use specific questions. Early in an interview, open-ended questions are better since they convey the least information to the member being interviewed about what you think. Later on you can get more specific, but be careful not to put words into the interviewee's mouth, regardless of what kind of question you ask.

Listening Well

The last major activity you need to perform in order to be a good interviewer is to listen well. This, along with being prepared, establishing a good atmosphere, and asking the right questions will produce the desired results leaders need in order to be successful in interviewing.

Whole books have been written on the subject of listening well because it is so important, and because we often do not do a particularly good job of doing it. Before you skip to the next chapter, thinking that you are not having a problem with listening well, please read the next two paragraphs.

Unless a person has a physical ear problem he can hear, and since we use our hearing all day long, it is natural to think that we do it well. So why is it necessary to talk about listening? The answer is quite simple. Hearing and listening are not the same thing. Hearing means to have the capacity of apprehending or perceiving sound, while listening is more than that; it is to pay thoughtful attention to that sound.

An example which shows the difference between hearing and listening takes place when a person is watching television. Someone will enter the room and ask the TV watcher to do something. The response is either "OK" or "In a minute" showing that sound was perceived—heard. An hour later the person who made the request reenters the room and finds that the television watcher has not moved an inch. The ensuing conversation goes something like this: "Didn't I ask you to take out the trash, since the garbage man was coming soon?" "I'm sorry. I didn't hear you." "What do you mean you didn't hear me? You answered and said you would do it in just a minute. You heard me just fine."

The person watching the television did hear the request to take out the trash. We are sure of that since the person even said, "In a minute." But what is just as evident is that listening did not take place. No thoughtful attention was given to what the person who requested that the garbage be taken out was saying. Instead, the person watching TV was focusing his attention and listening only to the tube.

This same situation happens all the time as we talk with other people. The only difference is that instead of a television set capturing our listening ear as the other person talks to us, it is our own mind that is holding our thoughtful attention.

Let's examine how this works. Imagine that you are talking to someone who is explaining something. If you are like most people, one of two things is happening. Either you are very interested in the topic, in which case your mind is racing ahead of the other person's words. Your thoughtful attention—listening—is focusing on similar experiences youhave had, things you have read, seen and heard on the subject and you become anxious to jump into the discussion and tell what you are thinking, or you are not interested in the topic in which case your mind and thoughtful attention are elsewhere as you dream dreams or plan plans a thousand miles away. This can be embarrassing when the other person suddenly asks you a question and you don't have the slightest idea what he was saying. You heard the sound of his voice, but you were listening to your thoughts, not to what he was saying.

When interviewing, there is a continuing danger that we will slip into this hearing-but-not-listening trap. It is very easy to do, especially if we are trying to think of what to next ask the interviewee. We will still be hearing, but we will not be listening well.

The solution is, first, recognize how often you slip into this habit and, second, concentrate on keeping your mind focused on what the person is saying—thoughtfully paying attention to what is said. To do this, you must have questions prepared ahead of time. You must also force yourself to be more interested in listening to what the other person says than in what you have to say. By doing these things you will become a better listener, and thereby a much better interviewer. You will also be amazed at how much better a conversationalist you will become by listening well.

Taking Notes

Just a word on taking notes during a church interview. Some people consider it inappropriate but that idea is incorrect. There are times when you must take very careful, accurate notes, such as during a church court—much of which is really an interview. There are other times when it would be very helpful, and would improve the interview process to take notes, such as when a priesthood leader or Relief Society presidency member interviews home or visiting teachers about their families. Of course there are also times when it would be better not to take notes at all during the interview.

The taking of notes during an interview in a court situation is quite obvious, but in what other interviews is note-taking appropriate? The general rule is to take notes only when specific information is being given which is important, which must be remembered in exact terms, and which could be forgotten if you do not write it down during the meeting. Do not take notes about information which is interesting but not critical to be remembered in its entirety. Also, except during church courts, do not take notes during confessions and other very personal discussions with members except in the very rarest of situations when it might be appropriate. When in doubt as to whether you should take notes or not . . . don't.

In most interviews the best approach is to listen well during the meeting without taking notes. After the meeting is over and you are alone, write brief notes which will help you remember the most important ideas and information you obtained.

We will now go on to the next chapter which deals with counseling members. As you will see, counseling uses many of the techniques and skills we have been talking about in this chapter on interviewing, since in many ways a counseling session is a form of an interview.

Chapter 8

Counseling

As Christians, we firmly believe in Christ's admonition referred to in the scriptures as being our brother's keeper. We care about— and for—one another, we care about assisting the sick, the widowed, the downtrodden, and the struggling members of the Church. The LDS welfare system is well-known and highly admired, especially since we do everything ourselves. We also try to consider the total person: the physical, social, emotional, mental, and spiritual needs of each individual.

This belief in assisting our brothers and sisters in every way possible causes church leaders to spend a large portion of their time working with members. Much of that time is spent counseling with individuals, couples, and families. But this counseling should not be confined just to bishops and branch presidents. Many members regularly have the chance to help other people through callings in class and quorum presidencies, home and visiting teaching assignments, and the more obvious callings such as priesthood, Relief Society and other auxiliary, and unit leaders. For this reason, it is imperative that members understand both the LDS philosophy behind counseling and how to do it effectively. This chapter will cover both these points.

LDS Philosophy in Counseling

A definite philosophy exists in the Latter-day Saint Church regarding counseling. At the foundation of that philosophy are several basic principles which govern the way we view ourselves and our fellow citizens here on earth. These basic principles explain and define the philosophy of counseling, so let's briefly consider each of them. Once we have a better understanding of what we hope to achieve through counseling, we will be ready to discuss the five major steps which should be followed in order to counsel effectively.

Help People to Help Themselves

At the very core of the philosophy of counseling is the idea that what we really want is for people to learn to independently stand on their own two feet; to be self-sufficient and to learn to deal with their own problems. But just as an eleven-month-old child needs help and support in learning to walk and to stand alone, church members also need help and support from time to time throughout their lives as they face the trials and learn the lessons of living in mortality.

A major challenge in counseling is to help other people without either doing all the work for them, or assuming all of the responsibility for the situation or problem. An example will help explain this concept. A young couple in financial trouble comes to you as bishop. After talking with them it becomes clear that they do not know how to keep their checkbook balanced, and they have not worked out a financial budget to guide them in their spending. Since both of these problems can be corrected, wouldn't it be good to either personally balance their checkbook and work out a reasonable budget for them, or get someone else to do these two things for them (since you have already read my chapter on delegating)? Wrong! You do not do the work; nor do you have it done for them. You have the young couple do these things themselves under the watchful eye of a knowledgeable person in your ward or branch to whom you delegate this assignment. You help the young couple to help themselves which gets at the root of the problem, and thereby permits real change and growth to take place.

If I had learned this principle of helping people to help themselves earlier in my own church life, I would certainly have saved hundreds of hours of my time. I would have also been much more effective in helping the members with whom I counseled. What I learned was that when people keep coming back time and time again for the same problem, two possible things are happening. Either the help they are getting is not involving them and therefore not encouraging them to assume ownership of the problem—by doing something about it themselves—or they just refuse to follow counsel and direction given. If it is the first reason, get them involved in helping themselves. If it is the second reason of refusing to accept responsibility to help themselves, do not spend hour after hour giving such members the same advice over and over again. We help an eleven-month-old child to walk by holding him as he tries very hard himself. If he were to just sit there and not try, our holding him up would not be of much value. Likewise, members must be willing to put forth the effort to help themselves, otherwise our effort to hold them up will be largely ineffective.

Avoid the Dole

An easy definition of the dole is "getting something for nothing." This idea goes against our LDS philosophy and tradition since we believe that it is unhealthy for people to be given the necessities of life without having to work for them. The dignity of the individual is only maintained, and the full value of items really appreciated, when we have worked for them ourselves and earned them. The dole takes away people's individual dignity and appreciation for the worth of things.

The reason for mentioning the importance of avoiding the dole, as part of our LDS philosophy relating to counseling, is because many situations arise during counseling where the leader could give something for nothing. Giving welfare assistance in the form of food or paying someone's bills is the most obvious example. Although we happily help worthy LDS individuals and families with such assistance—when all other means of help have first been fully explored— we must make sure we don't give assistance to them without their working for it in some way. It could mean the family washing the church windows, weeding the church lawn, or working at the welfare farm but some work must be agreed upon during the counseling discussion with the individual or family before assistance is given.

Another form of the dole is when we give advice and counsel without the member having to do anything except sit and listen. Counseling requires active participation by both parties in order to be successful. This can be accomplished by getting the member to discuss the issue, recognize the problem, think of solutions, and plan and commit to specific ways to improve and change. A successful leader will usually have to participate and guide the counseling session to accomplish this goal, but it can be done and the dole avoided. How to do this will be discussed later in this chapter. What is important now is to understand the concept of avoiding the dole when counseling.

Free Agency

In counseling with members we should remember that the person always maintains the right to accept or reject our counsel. He is free to follow what is considered the Lord's way, spoken through duly called representatives, or to ignore and even reject the direction offered.

As leaders, our responsibility when counseling is two-fold: it is to provide assistance in helping members to choose and follow correct paths, and to indicate consequences they will face by choosing various options. But it remains the member's right to choose which path to follow. Even though it may almost kill us to see someone pick the wrong road to follow—a road which will surely lead to misery and eternal unhappiness—we must respect the member's right of free agency to do so. And how great will be our joy when members pick those paths which lead to eternal happiness!

Maintain Dignity of Individual

When a member discusses difficult personal problems in a counseling situation—problems such as financial, moral, marital, testimony, doctrinal, or job related—it can cause that member great embarrassment and loss of self-esteem. In such instances, members may even feel unworthy and ashamed to associate with other members. During such traumatic situations, it is very important for the member to feel that someone cares about him as a person, and as a child of God. We can hate and abhor the sin, but we must love the sinner as our own closest brother or sister. In this way, the eternal worth and dignity of the individual is kept in mind and there remains purpose and reason for repentance and growth.

Focusing on the enormous love the Father and the Son have for each of us, as well as helping people to help themselves, avoiding the dole, respecting someone's free agency, and other principles we will discuss in this chapter related to the LDS philosophy behind counseling are all principles which will help us, as leaders, to assure that the individual's dignity is maintained throughout the counseling process.

There have been references made in this book on maintaining in strict confidence much of what we, as leaders, hear. Almost nothing will destroy an individual's dignity faster than a leader who does not use great restraint in discussing confidential matters about that person. The best policy is when in doubt . . . don't.

Respect the Family Unit

The family unit is the basic and most important unit of the Church. Everything else is there to support the family. Counseling is also designed to support families and family members. Whenever possible, the head of the family should be involved in the counseling process since he (she, if no husband is in the home) remains accountable for the family's welfare. This participation may be direct or indirect depending on the circumstances but, if at all possible, involvement should take place since we have previously seen that accountability is nontransferable. In fact, it could be stated that the ultimate goal through counseling could well be to transfer responsibility back to the family unit as quickly as possible—recognizing that this will sometimes be impossible, but that it is a goal to work toward.

Total Forgiveness Possible Through Christ

Counseling may deal with issues such as finances, schooling, the professional job, or certain legal matters; subjects which do not normally require repentance as part of the solution to the problem or situation. But other issues do require repentance. Moral transgressions, many personal problems, doctrinal and testimony difficulties, marital and family problems, or troubles involving the laws of the land almost always require repentance as part of the total resolution of the difficulties. For these issues, it is important for the leader to understand the concept of total forgiveness.

The unpardonable sins are the denial of the Holy Ghost after having truly received it and the taking of innocent blood—murder—for which there is no forgiveness in this life. Heavenly Father has made provision, through the atonement of His Son Jesus Christ, for all other sins to be completely and totally forgiven upon compliance with the prescribed steps of repentance. This means that even rape, major theft, adultery, or an abortion performed by converts before their baptism can be fully and totally forgiven. Granted, in all these cases (except problems prior to baptism) part of the full repentance process required is excommunication. But faithfulness thereafter will eventually permit rebaptism and a total cleansing through our Savior's atonement.

The purpose of this discussion is to remind church leaders who counsel members that no matter how bad the sins are which the members confess, total forgiveness is possible by complying with the laws of full repentance. We must view all members as potential heirs of the highest degree of glory in the celestial kingdom, and of attaining exaltation. To do less would be to deny the full import of Jesus

Christ's infinite gift to mankind. (For additional information on this topic please see section III, chapters 9 and 10 of this book.)

Don't Compromise Gospel Principles

The last major principle which helps to form our LDS philosophy regarding counseling deals with the attitude and integrity of the leader. Gospel principles may not be compromised—ever—to any degree. Leaders must be very careful in counseling not to compromise these principles to make counseling sessions easier on himself or the member.

Paying a full tithing means 10 percent of our gross income, not some derived portion thereof, regardless of taxes, family finances, the number of children in the home, what a church official is supposed to have told someone or any other reasons. Recently committed adultery requires excommunication in order for rebaptism to completely cleanse the person. Disfellowshipment, or some other form of probation, is not sufficient. Welfare assistance may only be given to worthy members—worthy meaning tithe paying, active, supportive members—and as a last resort after all the family's and other resources have first been exhausted. Assistance should not be used as a means of reactivating people for two reasons: First, that is not its purpose; and second, in 95 percent of the cases it does not work in reactivating people regardless of what they promise you during counseling.

Are there ever exceptions to these rules? There might be, but they would be few and far between. Leaders should spend their counseling time complying with the laws of the gospel instead of looking for obscure exceptions which might exist. If we don't compromise gospel principles members will receive better and more just help, and wc will maintain the integrity necessary to be successful.

The seven principles just discussed form an overall philosophy for counseling which will guide and direct us as we meet with church members in numerous counseling situations. Now that this framework has been established, let's move on to specifically discuss how to effectively counsel with people in the five parts of a counseling session.

Five Steps In Counseling

Throughout our lives we have counseled with friends and family. Additionally, some of us have been in work situations where counseling was necessary in the work place. These experiences may have given us ideas on what to say and how to handle certain counseling situations. What most of us have not done is to develop an approach which we can use again and again with the confidence that it will work. This step-by-step approach to counseling is what we will now develop.

You will see that the steps are not revolutionary, but practical. When followed in order they really work. Furthermore, this systematic approach has been successfully used as a framework for counseling members with everything from moral or testimony problems to marriage and financial difficulties.

1. Define Situation Clearly

The first thing to establish when counseling is a clear definition of the problem or situation. Until this has been done nothing very productive can happen to resolve or change the situation.

If the member initiates the meeting, make sure the person clearly defines the problem. You will often need to use several follow-up questions (discussed in Chapter 7, on interviewing) to understand both the issue and the magnitude of the problem's importance or severity. For example, if the member says, "The reason I asked to talk to you is because I am having marital problems," you will have to probe more deeply in order to clearly define the situation. You might ask, "What kind of marital problems? How serious is the situation?" Or simply say, "Please give me more information so that I can clearly understand the situation."

When you, as a church leader, initiate the meeting because you know that there is a problem, you must be prepared to clearly define the situation. This usually requires that you have back-up information to support your statement since the better you can document that you know what you are talking about, the more likely will the member be to open up, admit the problem, and discuss it.

For example, if the member is not fulfilling his church calling very well you might say, "The purpose in our meeting together today is to discuss your calling. I have noticed that we have had to get a substitute teacher on short notice to teach your class three times in the last four weeks. Also, when I visited your class today you apologized to the class for not being very well prepared. Since I would like to help, could you please share with me how you feel about your calling and what is happening?" In this way, the member will recognize that you realize there are problems and will be more willing to discuss them with you.

Whether you or the member initiate the meeting, it is very important that you agree on what the situation or problem is before you try to deal with it. The best way to do this is to summarize by saying something like, "Would you agree that the problem (situation, challenge) you face is . . ." then restate what you think the problem is. This will eliminate misunderstandings and form a solid foundation as you move to the second step in counseling.

2. Agree On Importance Of Improving, Changing, Resolving Situation

Once you and the member have defined the situation or problem, the next key step is to get the member to agree with you on the importance of doing something about the situation. That might mean you agree that improvement is necessary, that changes must take place or that there are things that need to be resolved.

The major thrust behind the LDS philosophy of counseling is that members take responsibility for their own actions. In order to accomplish this, we must continually focus the direction of the counseling session back to the member, that it is the member who must accept accountability for what is happening in his life, and that he must agree to do something about it.

Until the person agrees on the importance of improving, changing, or resolving the situation, it would be a waste of time to try to decide how to correct the situation or problem. This is an important point often glossed over during counseling sessions, either because it seems obvious, or because it does put pressure on the member. Agreement by the member to change must be clearly established in order for success to be achieved through counseling.

There are several ways to get someone to agree to improve, change, adjust, or resolve a situation or problem. We will mention four methods.

1. Emphasize the importance of change as it relates to the person's own personal life, and that of his family.

2. Emphasize your high level of expectation in the person, that you are convinced the member can and will change, and that you will help the person to accomplish the change.

3. Indicate the important role the person plays in the ward/ branch or stake/district, and that other members—and the Lord— are relying on him.

4. Indicate consequences the member will face by not improving, changing, adjusting, or resolving the situation or problem. This is not meant to be a threat, but rather a clear definition of consequences based on the member's actions. These consequences could involve the person's growth, the member's family, finances, the laws of the land, or the person's standing in the Church.

Once you have clearly defined the problem, and gotten the member to recognize and commit to the importance of improving, changing, or resolving it, you are ready to move to the third step in counseling.

3. Discuss Options, Solutions, Plans To Resolve Situation

With the situation defined and the Church member in agreement as to the importance of changing or resolving the problem, the third step is to discuss various options, solutions, or plans which might help.

This third step is where the real work begins. This step is a preparation for the fourth step which is where the decisions are actually made. Remember that it is very important, during this third step, for you to involve the member in coming up with ideas of what to do to resolve the situation or problem.

As you begin step three, you will probably need more background information as to why the problem or situation exists so start by saying something like, "In order for you to resolve this issue, you will have to make some good decisions as to what to do. I want to help you in making those decisions. Share with me more background on this matter." Then, depending on the issue, ask specific questions in order for you and the member to see the situation in its entirety. Continue to ask follow-up questions until you have a clear understanding of what you are dealing with.

The major activity in this step of the counseling process is to identify courses of action which the member might take. Try to brainstorm here as much as possible, but don't evaluate or judge the merits of each idea. Just help the member think of as many options as possible. Let's look at how this might work with our example counseling session which involved a struggling teacher.

After having the teacher more fully discuss the background you say, "Let's look at possible solutions to this situation (problem). We won't evaluate ideas right now, we'll just think of as many as we can and decide which would be the best for you. How can we solve this problem?" The teacher might answer: "Release me. I'm sure there are more qualified people who could do this calling." Do not evaluate this suggestion. Just say, "That is one solution. What other solutions can you think of?" Be prepared with several positive ideas of your own to add: ideas such as prepare the lesson ahead of time, meet with a leader for more training, commit to not calling at the last minute saying "I'm unable to attend," meet with the librarian to get ideas for visual aids, and team-teach with an auxiliary leader for several weeks in order to gain ideas and confidence.

During step three, even if the member can not think of anything to do to solve or resolve the situation and you have to think of all of the ideas, the emphasis should still be placed on the member's accountability for the situation or problem. You are merely assisting by thinking of ways the person can resolve his own problems. This emphasis will become even more obvious to the member as you move on to step number four in counseling. In summary, step number three is where various ideas are developed as to how to change or resolve the situation or problem with emphasis remaining on the person to be accountable for his own life.

4. Decide on Solutions, Plans To Resolve Situation

We have now reached the point in counseling where leaders traditionally have the most difficulty, that of deciding what to do to change or resolve the situation and in getting the member to agree to the plan. But by using the first three counseling steps recommended, this fourth step becomes much easier. It is a natural outgrowth of groundwork already established.

The best way to start number four is to remind the member— and yourself—of what has already been accomplished. You might begin by summarizing: "Thus far we have defined the situation (problem), you agreed to change (resolve, improve), and we identified a number of possible things to do in order to accomplish that goal. Do you agree?" Make sure the member does agree before you continue with the fourth step in counseling. If, for some reason, he does not agree, resolve areas of disagreement before proceeding with step four.

After you have agreed on what has been accomplished, move right into the main objective of step four which is for the member to decide which ideas should be implemented in order to solve or change the problem or situation. The person should choose from ideas the two of you discussed in step three. These decisions will often be clear and straightforward. If you feel that the decisions are obvious and that the member will probably choose good action plans, ask the person to decide on what to do.. You might say, "We have made good progress in identifying good ideas on how to change (resolve, solve) the situation (problem). Now you need to decide which of these ideas you are going to use to correct (resolve, change) the problem (situation)." Then wait for the person to decide.

When decisions are not quite so obvious, or when the member may not choose the best plans to resolve the situation you should begin the selection process. Do this by eliminating one or two ideas the member might pick, but which would clearly not be good choices. For example, in the case of the struggling teacher, you might say, "We have made good progress in identifying several good ideas as to how to change (resolve, solve) the situation (problem). From what you have said about problems with your teaching assignment, and the importance of your improving that calling, it has become obvious to me that we should eliminate the idea of just releasing you at this time. That is not the answer. So let's look at other ideas we thought of. Which do you think will help you to be successful in your present calling?" Then wait for the member to think through the various ideas and come up with a constructive plan. The person might still ask to be released, but it is more likely that the member will follow your direction and choose positive ideas for improving.

As soon as the member identifies an idea which you think is positive, regardless of how major or minor the point is, reinforce that proper decision immediately. You might say, "That's a good idea. I agree that it should help you." Then ask the member to choose other ideas from those previously discussed, but be ready to jump in with one or two of your own if the person gets stumped. If the member has difficulty deciding you could ask, "I think the idea we mentioned earlier of asking the (auxiliary) counselor to work with you for the next several weeks is a good idea, and I'm sure he (she) will be happy to do it. Shall we include that on your list of good things to do?" After the person agrees, turn it back to him again by asking, "Which other ideas are you going to pick?" In this way you will help the person develop a list of several positive ideas for improving or resolving the situation or problem.

During this part of the counseling session, it is helpful for you to write down each of the ideas as the member and you decide on them. This adds importance to the ideas and will act as a "reminder list" (which we will discuss in step number five). In summary, step number four is where you help the member pick specific solutions to change or resolve the problem or situation.

5. Agree on Follow-up Actions and Timetable

Planning only produces results when the plans are implemented, and nowhere is this more true than in counseling. It is therefore crucial that follow-up actions and a timetable are agreed upon before the counseling session ends.

The first four counseling steps we have discussed are designed to help the Church member plan a course of action which will solve problems and resolve situations. If, after the counseling session ends, little of what was planned is actually implemented by the member, then the counseling can be considered ineffective and a waste of time in the long run. The purpose of this fifth and final step in a counseling session is to help insure that plans and ideas are actually implemented and not just talked about.

Most of us have good intentions to live as we should and do what is right. The challenge comes in our translating intentions into actions. We often tend to procrastinate implementing even very good action plans. Rather than discussing the possible reasons why we do this, let's just agree that this procrastination often happens and go on to consider how to help members with whom we counsel to avoid falling into this pattern of not following through.

The secret for success in helping members to follow through with implementing the plans we jointly develop is rather simple. It involves closely related activities on our part as the leader which we will now look at.

Reminder List: Before the member leaves the counseling session each of you has to be sure you know exactly what ideas or plans were agreed upon in step number four. Just to mention them again is not good enough. You should reread the list you just made and make sure the member still agrees to all the points. Then quickly rewrite the list and give a copy to the member. You must actually do this if you want to succeed! This list will act as a daily reminder to the person of the steps he agreed to during the session with you and it will become invaluable in helping the member to follow through on what you both discussed and decided.

Follow-up Actions and Dates: The "reminder list" can help the member, but it must have additional information in order to be most useful. Next to each idea or plan on the list there must be follow-up actions and dates. These represent agreed-upon times when the member will start, stop, or complete certain activities, then contact you to give a progress report. There is nothing like having to report back to someone on a specific item, at a definite date and time, to help persuade people to follow through, especially if the person knows that you have that same follow-up information on your copy of the list. The member should be told that you expect to hear from him on a specific day, and that, if you don't hear, you will call him.

Don't be bashful at this point in the counseling session as you will never have a better time to help the person by applying positive pressure for improvement. It is now that a friendly push is often needed to help get the procrastinating member off dead center, and moving in the right direction. The more specific you can be on follow-up actions, times, and dates, the greater the help you will be to the person. Of course you must follow through and actually call the member if he does not call you first. It is obvious that if you were to not follow through, you would lose much of your credibility as a leader. So put the information on your daily calendar, and follow through. In summary, the final step in a counseling session is to agree on specific follow-up actions, with dates and times for the member to report back to you on his progress.

Closing a counseling session should be positive, encouraging and with prayer. Make sure to express your sincere appreciation for the member's having met with you.

Subsequent Counseling Sessions

Successful counseling often requires more than one meeting. Subsequent meetings are all right and even encouraged as long as they are done as prescribed in this chapter.

There are two reasons for holding a subsequent counseling session. One reason is to reinforce and congratulate the person for improvement and positive change. The other is to try to help the member who did not respond as hoped for and who failed to follow through on plans and commitments made in the first counseling session. Let's briefly consider each situation.

To Reinforce Success

To hold a second meeting with a member for the purpose of congratulations on successfully following through on plans or ideas is a positive, rewarding experience for both of you. Unfortunately, it does not happen as often as it should: not because members don't have success, but because leaders fail to recognize the importance of using this effective leadership technique to reinforce the member's accomplishments.

It's hard to find someone who does not like to be sincerely complimented and congratulated. Such treatment makes us feel good about ourselves. From a successful leader's standpoint, it also reinforces the positive, desirable behavior of the member. That is often critical in order for the member to sustain the positive change. And isn't it understandable for the member to hope for—and even expect—positive feedback and follow-up? Certainly it is. The member met with the leader. They discussed a personal situation or problem. The member decided on specific action plans to change or improve, promised to report back to the leader, and then—most importantly—followed through which is by far the hardest part. It would be surprising if such a member did not sincerely expect positive recognition from the leader.

When members do follow through after the first counseling session, make sure you meet with them as soon as possible to congratulate them and to reinforce positive actions they should continue. This meeting should not be long but it will pay handsome dividends both to the member and to the leader because of the reinforcing effect it will have.

To Further Encourage Improvement, Change

A reality in the life of all leaders, no matter how competent they are, is that some members who meet with them and go through the five counseling steps which we just discussed do not follow through. Some people make a valiant effort but fail, while a few don't even try. When this happens, it is necessary for the leader to try to meet a second time with the member in order to further encourage improvement and/or change.

One of the reasons that the five steps in counseling which are recommended here are particularly effective in helping people is because they lend themselves so well to these second and even third counseling sessions while maintaining the overall LDS philosophy which we said was so important. The reason for this effectiveness is that a second or third counseling session with the same person, regarding the same problem or situation, should merely be an extension of the first meeting. In that way, all the positive aspects of the first meeting are reinforced and further built upon. This method also most effectively strengthens the member's resolve to follow through. To better understand how this works, let's look at how a second or third counseling session should be handled.

When meeting for a second time with a member who did not follow through very well after his first counseling session, you should follow the same five-step format used before. You begin by again clearly defining the situation after which you briefly summarize what was agreed on during the last meeting. Then, since the member did not follow through as planned, it is vital that you reestablish the importance of the person's improving, changing, or resolving the situation or problem (step number 2). During this second meeting, you must more explicitly help the person recognize the likely consequences of his not improving or changing. If someone's continued membership in the Church is in jeopardy, then that must now be forcefully explained in no uncertain terms, since the person might not have fully understood the seriousness of the situation during the first meeting. If failure to change or improve will mean increased problems for the member—whether financial, marital, family, testimony, or others—now is the time to help the person recognize the real importance of improvement or change. Get the person to make a commitment to you that he understands the importance of, and is interested in, changing.

If this is the third meeting with the same person, for the same reason, then this second counseling step should be taken even further. You must explain that failure to change or improve will definitely—not maybe or probably—result in certain specific consequences. This should be your last attempt to help the member improve, change, or resolve the situation or problem. If, after three counseling sessions conducted as outlined in these pages, the person is still not changing, improving, or resolving the situation or problem, the leader should tell the member that no further help will be offered until some positive actions are taken by the member to resolve or change his own situation. At that point the leader should also take whatever church actions are appropriate for the situation.

During the second and the third session, after counseling step number two is clearly covered and agreed to, move on to the last three steps which are to discuss possible solutions, then decide on specific solutions and finally agree on clear follow-up actions and a timetable. In most cases, the member will recognize the importance of changing and will apply ideas and plans you worked out together for that purpose.

Although a full book could be written on this subject of counseling in the LDS Church, the basic information of how to be successful as a church leader in counseling is contained in this chapter. There will undoubtedly be some situations you face which require a slightly modified approach. But by following the ideas presented here you will find that the vast majority of counseling situations you face will comfortably fit into the five key steps described here.

In conclusion, I found it very helpful to actually type these five counseling steps on a 3 × 5-inch card, and keep it with me during counseling sessions. It never seemed to bother the person with whom I met and it certainly helped remind me which step I was on and which step came next. That helped me to relax, to listen better, and to think more about what was being said and what to say, rather than to worry about what to do next.

Five Steps in Counseling

1. *Define situation* clearly

2. *Agree on importance of improving,* changing situation

3. *Discuss options,* solutions, plans

4. *Decide on solutions,* plans

5. *Agree on follow-up actions and timetable*

Section III
A Foundation Of Rock

Introduction

One of the most famous parables the Savior used is found in Matthew, chapter seven. It is the story of two men who built homes—one built on sand and the other built on rock. We are not told what the houses looked like but I imagine them to have been lovely homes. Detailed blueprints could have been used. Craftsmen of great skill might have applied their vast experience in creating those lovely dwellings. My imagination envisions perfectly formed archways, great towers, massive walls, and rich marble floors. Years of expert labor could have been required to complete the construction. After all of this, and in spite of it, one of the houses could not withstand the storms which invariably came and beat upon it; "and great was the fall of it" (verse 27).

A number of parallels can be drawn between the account of the two houses and the success we have in positions of responsibility in the church. This book deals with improving our abilities in church leadership. To that end, this section discusses the foundation upon which all the rest must be built in order for us to have lasting stability and real success as leaders. Without this foundation we will not be able to weather life's storms. We might build beautiful structures, devote tremendous amounts of time and energy to what we do and become genuinely proficient in carrying out our callings, but without a proper foundation the most splendid palace on earth will, in time, crumble.

What is this all important foundation upon which we should build our church leadership qualities and abilities? I call it *Personal Spirituality.*

Realizing that many books have been written which deal with the spiritual side of being a good Latter-day Saint, I have concentrated on four principle areas which church leaders should consider. Each of these topics is discussed by using church leadership situations and examples, and helps direct us toward personal spirituality.

Chapter 9

Repentance

Making an exquisite, priceless vase of rare quality is something only the finest of master potters can accomplish. Such works of art require the very finest clay as the raw material used by the artist. With such clay, the master craftsman can shape and mold and form whatever he desires. The only limitations are those imposed by the quality of the clay itself. Knowing this, the potter selects the clay with great care, ever alert to imperfections which the master knows must be removed before his work of art is fired. If the clay will not withstand the intense heat it will not become a masterpiece. The refiner's fire will not overlook imperfections.

After careful selection of the clay, and to insure success, the master craftsman spends a great deal of time working the clay. In the potter's hands, this working of the clay may include pounding, pulling, plucking out, stroking and smoothing. Water may be added to soften the clay to make it respond more easily to the artist's touch. Impurities are removed from the clay little by little, first the obvious imperfections then, increasingly, the subtle and small ones. In time, after much effort and care by the craftsman, the clay is completely free of impurities; it is finally ready for the master to make of it that priceless treasure.

In ancient Israel, the making of clay pottery was a commonplace occurrence. Kowing this, the great prophet Isaiah used the example of the potter and clay as he prayed for the return of God's mercy to Israel. In his prayer, Isaiah identifies the Lord as being the potter, and our father. We are referred to as being the clay; the work of His hand. "But now, O Lord, Thou art our father; we are the clay, and thou our potter; and we all are the work of thy hand." (Isaiah 64:8.) We are the clay in the hands of the greatest master craftsman of them all: the Lord Himself. We are His creation and Isaiah correctly refers to Him as our father. Modern scriptures further explain that it is His work and glory to make of us His greatest masterpieces; to make us immortal, with eternal life, and eventually even as He is.

Using Isaiah's metaphor that we are the clay and God is the potter, let us consider the implications. We have seen that imperfect clay full of impurities cannot, in that state, produce masterpieces even in the hands of a great artist. The master must first purify the clay by removing the imperfections. Similarly, in each of our lives, there are impurities and imperfections. These must be removed before our Father can complete His work and make of us a masterpiece. We will not be able to withstand the refiner's fire if impurities remain.

Personal spirituality cannot be fully attained, or maintained, when there are impurities in our lives. We are told by the Lord that the Holy Ghost will not dwell with us as long as we are unclean; meaning living in sin. He will depart from us. The only way to cleanse the clay is to remove the impurities. It takes hard work, time, and rigid dicipline to accomplish this goal. Removing our own personal impurities requires no less effort. Only after complete repentance can we expect to fully receive the promised blessings of the Lord.

Let's look at an example of differences complete repentance can make in the attitude and functioning of a church leader. John, a counselor in an elders quorum presidency, had committed a transgression which was serious enough that complete repentance required confession to his Bishop. It was not so serious that automatic disfellowshipment or excommunication would result, but it was serious. John had fulfilled all of the other steps in repenting as best he could. Confession, however, and its possible consequences, had frightened him into silence. This situation undermined the counselor's foundation of personal spirituality, and that affected John's whole administration in the elders quorum.

Lack of Repentance Causes Leadership Problems

At least six specific problems related to church leadership resulted from John's lack of complete repentance.

First

John's prayers were continually apologetic, especially his personal prayers. His supplications were filled with themes such as; "Please help me, in spite of my unrepented sins, for the members' sake."

Second

John knew well the verses in the 130th section of the Doctrine and Covenants which say that irrevocable laws in heaven exist upon which all blessings are predicated. "And when we obtain any blessing from God, it is by obedience to that law upon which it is predicated" (verse 21). When we are called to church leadership positions we need all the blessings we can get. To know that by our own disobedience, we are not permitting ourselves to receive needed blessings is disheartening and frustrating.

Third

Another problem John faced was knowing that he needed the guidance and influence of the Holy Ghost in order to fulfill his calling properly. But he also knew that the Spirit of the Lord would not dwell in unholy temples. John's anxieties were heightened even more as he was called upon to give blessings, perform priesthood administrations, and seek counsel of the Spirit. He silently worried: "How can I do these things if the Spirit of the Lord is not with me? Will I be helped for the members' sake, but will it be a curse to me?"

Fourth

Feeling like a hypocrite was another problem caused by lack of total repentance. It was important, John felt, to stand before the members and exhibit confidence and ability, yet spirituality and humility. He conducted meetings, bore his testimony, and taught lessons, all the while feeling that he was cheating the Lord and being dishonest to the members.

Fifth

An uneasy, unsure feeling about his church calling also existed within John due to lack of confirmation of the Spirit that the things he was doing and saying were really the will of Heavenly Father.

Sixth

The final problem area was simply a question in John's mind as to what opportunities, blessings, experiences, and callings might have passed him by and been given to another more worthy than he.

The Miracle

John's decision to set his own house in order by strengthening his personal foundation of spirituality through complete repentance did not occur in one day. This is a good example of how the Lord refuses to give up on us often, it seems, in spite of ourselves. The impact of the six specific problems just discussed certainly contribbuted to John's decision to fully repent. John's recognition that total repentance was the only way to gain complete forgiveness and peace of mind finally brought him to the point of making the decision to talk to his bishop. He then prayed to the Lord for the confirmation that this decision was correct. The more John prayed, the stronger a desire within him grew to go and confess and be done with it once and for all. A vision of cleanliness and freedom from sin washed away brought excitement to John's whole soul. He could not wait to go and do what he knew to be right.

As John left the bishop's office, with eyes still wet and a tight throat, his steps seemed to flow effortlessly along the church's hallway. Being alone, he moved very, very slowly, still transfixed with the spirit he felt. There was love and warmth and compassion, and most of all absolute and unequivocal forgiveness. The Lord's own words, spoken by a loving bishop, kept playing over and over again in his mind: "Though your sins be as scarlet I will make them white as snow, and I the Lord will remember them no more." His gratitude for the Savior, and what He personally did for John, made the tears start to unashamedly flow again.

Now let's contrast the problems and negative feelings John felt earlier with what he experienced after completely repenting. It becomes apparent that one's capabilities to lead and direct in the Church are enhanced immensely through the process of sincere and total repentance.

In contrast to the six problem areas John experienced earlier related to church leadership, he could now build upon a solid base. His prayers became positive petitions for help and guidance, knowing that he was doing all that he could. Not apologetic now, but with sincere supplications to an accepting Father, the themes of John's prayers became; "I am the workable, willing clay in thine hands, thy will be done." His whole attitude was different now; he felt good about himself. The scripture which says: "If ye love me, keep my commandments," was not a millstone around his neck pulling him down. It had become a positive statement that the counselor felt applied specifically to his situation. John was showing the Lord that he really did love Him. These positive, worthy feelings made acceptance by Heavenly Father, and help through the Holy Ghost, seem to be within John's reach. And they were, now. He could enjoy the spiritual blessings of inspiration, insight, direction, impressions, and sensitivities all of which are necessary in order to be really successful as a church leader.

Repentance, then, is one of the most vital elements necessary for success as a church leader. It is a prerequisite to building the foundation of personal spirituality. It is the method by which impurities and imperfections are removed from us—the potter's clay. Through it, we can become priceless possessions in the Master's hands. It is not the purpose of this book to go into further detail regarding repentance, but only to show that it is indispensable in the lives of church leaders. The book, *The Miracle of Forgiveness*, by our beloved Prophet Spencer W. Kimball, is truly a classic work on the subject of repentance. Studying this book is highly recommended to further strengthen church leaders and to help them in the many counseling situations they face where repentance is the fundamental issue.

Chapter 10

Obedience

Obedience is the second critical quality necessary for us to build our own secure foundation of personal spirituality. It is the quality or state of being in compliance with, and submissive to, all the laws and ordinances of the gospel of Jesus Christ.

By strict obedience to the gospel it is not necessary to go through the various steps of repentance for sin, since where there is no disobedience, there is no sin. Repentance cleanses us, obedience keeps us clean. Do not misunderstand; today's obedience will not remove yesterday's transgressions any more than not getting dirtier today automatically eliminates the unwashed filth of yesterday.

Obedience To the Laws Of the Gospel

Obedience covers several areas, and in order to be effective church leaders each of these must be observed. The first is obedience to the laws and commandments of the restored gospel of Jesus Christ. Such laws as tithing, the Word of Wisdom, moral cleanliness, keeping the Sabbath day holy, and honesty are some of the commandments we must faithfully observe. With few exceptions, members know what the laws and commandments are. We don't need to have a long list presented to us. We know which ones we are obeying and which we are not obeying. We know where our obedience is not what it should be, and where we should improve. Our real challenge is to do something about it. The problem is often lack of commitment—real commitment to change.

A young man once went to his bishop and, in tears, confessed to a continuing problem of masturbation. After talking together for a few minutes, the bishop perceived several things. One was that, to the young man, the seriousness of this transgression was not in proper perspective with other sins. The young man said, "When I became a Mormon I committed to myself and to Heavenly Father never to drink even one sip of coffee again." He continued, "I have not had any and I will not, even if it means threats of cutting off my arms, or being shot, I will not drink coffee!" A little melodramatic, but he really was serious. This teenager had made an irrevocable decision with a commitment in his own mind never to drink coffee again. It was not a topic for discussion or consideration as far as he was concerned.

When challenged never to masturbate again, the young man said, "I'll try. I'll really try not to." The difference in level of commitment became obvious immediately. Trying not to sin is better than not trying, but trying does not carry the same definite resolve as an irrevocable, once and for all, final decision in one's mind that it cannot, and will not ever, ever happen again.

The young man had been entertaining thoughts which were impure, looking at pictures and movies which were suggestive, and placing himself in situations of being alone where such desires could easily be fulfilled. He had not learned the simple truth that most people are not strong enough to continually withstand certain temptations if they are constantly placed before them. You have to learn to run from such situations as did David of old. The temptation will differ from person to person. Each of us has our own particular challenges and in order to be consistently obedient we must be wise enough to know what our weaknesses are, to shun them, and to run from them.

Obedience To Covenants We Have Made

The second area of obedience is closely related to the first: We must be obedient to the covenants we have made with the Lord. At the time of baptism we promised Heavenly Father to remember to keep the commandments established by Jesus Christ, and to observe the laws of the church. These covenants we make at baptism are to be renewed weekly as we take the bread and water of the sacrament. In the prayers offered as these emblems are blessed, we say that we again witness to, or covenant with, God the Father that we will remember Jesus Christ, take upon us the Savior's name, and keep His commandments. Making such covenants, and reaffirming them weekly, commits us to full repentance and puts us under solemn obligation to be totally obedient.

Additionally, specific covenants are required of us as we receive the Holy Ghost by the laying on of hands, receive the priesthood with accompanying oaths and covenants, go to a holy temple and receive our own endowment, are married or sealed for all eternity, and accept important leadership positions in the Church. By accepting such covenants, and then living them, we strengthen our personal spirituality.

Obedience To Presiding Leaders

The third area of obedience we must observe as church leaders is that of being obedient to those in authority who have been called to preside over us and over our stewardships. There are two distinct groups of church leaders whom we must obey, so we will discuss them separately.

Each of us lives in a ward or branch, and stake or district. Our children attend Sunday School and Primary, and participate in youth activities. Our sons, age twelve and over, and the brethren, are members of priesthood quorums. The sisters are members of the Young Women's program or Relief Society. In a word, we are members in a number of church organizations, classes and quorums where other people have been called to preside over us. This is true of all of us in the Church, regardless of our own church positions and callings, or those of our spouses. In the hierarchy of the Church, we and our families are to be subject to our local leaders as these leaders direct us in righteousness.

An example of how this works will help clarify this principle. Let us consider a counselor in a stake presidency. Even though he participated in the calling of key ward officers, he is still a member of his own ward and must be interviewed by his bishop in order to renew his temple recommend. Also, he is assessed an annual ward budget amount by his bishop. The stake presidency member is assigned a home teaching companion and families to home teach by the ward high priest group leader—after bishopric approval—and meets monthly to report on his home teaching stewardship either with his ward high priest group leader or an assistant group leader. In his own ward, the counselor in the stake presidency and his family are to be obedient to those ward leaders who have been called to preside over them.

The hierarchical reporting relationships within the Church produce the second distinct group of church leaders to whom we must be obedient. Simply stated, each church leader reports directly to someone and is expected to follow the righteous counsel and direction of the individual to whom he reports. A Primary teacher reports to a counselor in the Primary presidency, who in turn reports to the Primary president, who then reports to a counselor in the bishopric, who reports to the bishop, who then reports to the stake president, who reports to the regional representative, and so on all the way to the living prophet.

Obedience, then, is the second important principle which helps our personal spirituality. We have defined obedience as: (1) Keeping the laws and commandments of the gospel; (2) Being true to the covenants we have made; (3) Obeying and supporting church leaders.

Chapter 11

Prayer

First, let's put prayer into proper perspective. If you were asked, as a church leader, "What do you need in order to fulfill your calling?" what one word would pop into your mind? For many of us that word would be "help": all the help we can get. We are often overwhelmed by the magnitude of what is expected of us and what we need to do. We are asked to make very difficult decisions which almost always affect the lives of other people. Our church positions require talents, skills and abilities which we often do not have. Yes, we need all the help we can get if we are to be successful church leaders. Prayer is the means by which we can receive much of that help.

To better understand the importance of prayer, let's take the example of a branch president whose executive secretary had scheduled three meetings for him on a certain Wednesday night. The branch president had previously instructed his executive secretary to always try to gently direct members who want to see him to see their appropriate priesthood leader first—except, of course, on moral issues. This is a very delicate job for the executive secretary. He can't ask the members the subject they wish to discuss with the president, nor can he make it sound as if the branch president is not interested in seeing people. The executive secretary might have said something such as, "I am sure President Smith would be happy to meet with you. Since he is such a busy person I try to encourage members to meet with their priesthood leaders instead of the president, wherever possible. Would you like me to set up a meeting for you to see Brother Anderson (the person's priesthood leader), or with President Smith?" On this particular Wednesday evening, the three meetings were with members who had asked specifically to meet with the branch president.

The first meeting was with a thirty-five-year-old woman whom the branch president had only met once before when he visited at her small apartment. In getting background information prior to the Wednesday evening meeting at his office, the branch president had determined several facts. She almost never attended church. Her four pre-teen children attended Sunday School and Primary sporadically. She did not pay any tithes or offerings, was not married, and had been seen smoking by branch members. Both the home teachers and the visiting teachers reported that they had not been able to meet with her in the last several months. She and her two older children were baptized members.

As the woman explained her problems of being out of work, being a month behind with her rent, and having no food for the children, the branch president thought to himself; "Help! Now what do I do?" She was clearly not worthy to receive church welfare assistance, but what about the little children? Should he show compassion or be tough on this member; send her to government welfare agencies, try to get distant relatives involved, turn the whole thing over to the branch priesthood leaders and Relief Society, or go ahead and give her church welfare? The branch president clearly needed guidance and direction from the Lord, both in what he said and how he said it. He thought to himself, "I prayed to the Lord to please bless me this evening with His Spirit, and to let me know what to say and do during these meetings. I certainly need that help now." Almost as he thought this to himself the branch president could feel a peace and assurance come over him, a knowledge of what to say and do.

First, find out how much food there really was. There was enough for a day or two. Good. Then talk about her relatives and insist that they get involved right away. Get names, addresses, and telephone numbers. Next, talk about part-time job opportunities which she could start immediately. After that, talk about how you want to get the priesthood leaders and the Relief Society involved in following through with her. The home teacher should talk to the landlord about the overdue rent and ask for a little more time to pay it. Then end with a discussion about the Church. Get her to commit to attending meetings, starting at once, and no more cigarettes. She will never be more willing to really try than now. Also, reinforce her need for blessings and explain the law of the tithe. Close with prayer, even a special bishop's blessing if she wishes. The branch president was grateful for the insight and direction he felt as he started outlining what needed to be done, all without the use of church funds. His prayer had been answered.

The second meeting that night involved a man with a morality problem he wanted to confess. Decisions needed to be made by the branch president as to whether or not a court was required. What should be said to this man? How were both justice and mercy to be satisfied? Again, the president clearly needed help from the Lord to guide what he did and said. The meeting went well.

After waiting fifteen minutes past the appointed hour for the third meeting the branch president telephoned the member's home to see if there was a problem. The member had forgotten that the meeting was that night. A new meeting would be scheduled by the executive secretary. Before leaving the church building, the branch president knelt and thanked Heavenly Father for the gospel of Jesus Christ. He was grateful for the influence and direction he had received from the Lord and for the sustaining power of the Holy Ghost. He was thankful for the possibility to talk with Heavenly Father through prayer and for the testimony which burned within him that such prayers really were answered.

This example of a branch president meeting with members in need is repeated hundreds—probably thousands of times each day around the world. God certainly is totally aware of the needs of these leaders. Whether it is a difficult counseling situation, as were the two examples just mentioned, or any number of other duties church leaders must perform, the principles are the same. The Lord is well aware of our needs, even before we ask. (3 Nephi 13:8.) That does not change our responsibility to ask Him in order to receive the help we need. Repeatedly, the scriptures indicate that God stands at the door waiting for us to seek, to knock, and to ask. As we exercise our faith, and ask, we shall receive.

What Help Can We Receive Through Prayer?

A good question one might ask regarding prayer is, "Exactly what can we, as leaders, expect to receive in the way of help, through prayer?" When the Lord does reveal His will on matters which have worldwide or churchwide implications, He always does it through His living prophet.

The kind of help we should expect to receive as a result of our fervent prayers is confined to our specific needs and to our areas of responsibility. Within those parameters, however, the help we can receive is far beyond most of our understanding. We have already seen the example of how a branch president was given insight and clear direction concerning a difficult welfare matter. Help of this kind is received daily by thousands of church members as they faithfully keep the commandments and strive to serve their Eternal Father. Such help is certainly not confined to members in leadership positions. All of us are entitled to the help of the Lord if we will do those things upon which His blessings are based.

Five Requirements For Prayers To Be Answered

What are those steps which must be taken in order to receive answers to our prayers? The Lord tells us there are laws upon which the receiving of blessings is predicated. That means these laws are eternal in nature and do not change. As we study the scriptures pertaining to this matter, we find that at least five specific requirements exist which must be fulfilled in order for our prayers to be answered. When we meet these criteria, we receive the accompanying blessing or help. When the prerequisites are not met, the blessing is not given. Let us briefly consider what these five laws are.

Obedience

Obedience, which we have already discussed, is certainly one of the factors necessary for us if we are to receive, by the power of the Holy Ghost, direction and help from God. Heavenly Father says that He is bound when we do what He says, but that we have no such promise when we do not do what He says. (D & C 82:10.)

Faith

A second requirement is faith. We must ask in faith. The passage of scripture in James which had such a profound impact on young Joseph Smith states that God will give wisdom to all men who ask of Him. It is significant to note, however, that the author of that famous verse immediately continues with the clear, specific, and repeated direction that he who asks must do so in unwavering faith. (James 1:5-7.) It is that mighty faith, not just the lack of wisdom, which is a key by which prayers are answered.

Do Our Part

Besides obedience and unwavering faith, another necessary criterion is the need for us to do our part, to do all that we can before we go to the Lord in prayer for help. Earlier in this book we discussed a clear explanation of this principle which was given by the Lord through Joseph Smith to Oliver Cowdery in April of 1829. It stated that we have to study the matter out first, pondering it in our mind, then make a decision after which we ask, in prayer, whether the decision is correct. If it is right, we will know that it is. If our decision is not right, then we will know that it is not correct. (D&C) 9:7-9.)

The Lord's Will

The fourth important requirement regarding prayer is that it be the will of the Lord that our prayers be answered at that time. It may not fit into Heavenly Father's plans, either for us or for others involved, that He make His will known to us then and there. In section 42 of the Doctrine and Covenants, the Lord speaks of our receiving blessings such as revelation, knowledge, and mysteries unfolded. He then makes an interesting statement through the Prophet Joseph Smith: "Thou shalt ask, and it shall be revealed unto you in mine own due time where the New Jerusalem shall be built." (D & C 42:62.) "In mine own due time" may not always be the time frame we had in mind. This is where faith, and being close to the Spirit of the Lord, will help us to accept those things which we do not fully understand. Our attitude in these cases has to echo the words of the Savior as He said; ". . . thy will be done." (Matt. 26:42.)

In Fervent Prayer

The fifth requirement necessary in order for our prayers to be answered is that our supplicatons to the Lord be done in a manner which James called; "The effectual fervent prayer." (James 5:16.) The word "fervent" has its roots in the Latin verb *fervere*, which means to boil. When we think of something boiling, we usually associate it with intense heat or with something in a very active state. James' choice of words becomes highly descriptive of the effort, or intensity, which he felt was involved in effective prayers. Other words with similar meanings could be substituted for "fervent." As Moroni, the last great prophet of the Book of Mormon, ended his writings he exhorted us to first read the record and then to pray to God the Eternal Father in order that we might know that the things which were written were true. Moroni says that we must pray with a sincere heart, with faith in Christ, and with real intent. (Moroni 10:4.) By saying "with real intent," Moroni was conveying the same idea as James did when he used the word "fervent," in referring to prayer.

Another Book of Mormon example involves the conversation of the King of the Land of Nephi. As the King accepted Aaron's preaching, he bowed down in prayer, the King "cried mightily" unto God and sought forgiveness, to be born of God, and to receive the Lord's Spirit. (Alma 22:15-17.) Whether we call it "fervent prayer," "with real intent," or "crying mightily unto God," the meaning is the same. We must pray with real intensity if we are to receive help from the Lord.

Prayer then, is an indispensable part of good church leadership, and the means by which we can receive much needed help from the Lord. No decisions, actions or plans should ever be made without first humbly going to Heavenly Father in fervent prayer for His will to be made known to us. Prayer is vital to us as we build our foundation of personal spirituality.

Chapter 12

Gospel Study

Our goal is to be good church leaders. We have seen that to accomplish this it is necessary for our individual foundations to be built upon personal spirituality. Three ingredients which help form this personal spirituality have been discussed: repentance, obedience, and prayer. The fourth requirement to insure a firm foundation is regular study of the gospel.

Of the many positive reasons for going on a church mission, one of the most important is the opportunity to significantly strengthen our own testimonies. This is done as the truth is made manifest to us by the power of the Holy Ghost. Where does the truth come from? It comes from the scriptures, other missionaries, our mission president, and from many experiences we have while in the mission field. But, most of all, the truth is made known to us by the Holy Ghost. We change from being unsure and tentative missionaries to being convinced and confident that the restored gospel is exactly what it claims to be.

How Study Builds the Foundation

My own experience with gospel study as a young missionary in Europe was probably not unlike that of thousands and thousands of other missionaries around the world. During the early 1960s there was no Language Training Mission where several weeks of gospel and language training took place. As new missionaries, we had one highly motivating week at the Mission Home in Salt Lake City. At the end of that week, we had the chance to bear our testimonies at a special testimony meeting held in the Assembly Hall on Temple Square. We were then sent out into the world to preach, teach, and baptize.

After arriving in Munich, West Germany, I met and visited with Mission President Owen Spencer Jacobs and his wife. Twenty-four hours later I was in a suburb of Munich with my companion, Elder

Reading who had been on his mission ten months. His attitude and enthusiasm were great, his German seemed very good, and it also seemed to me that he knew everything there was to know about the gospel.

On our third day of tracting without anyone inviting us in, a woman asked us into her home, saying that her husband would speak to us. Elder Reading did not have a chance to say two words to the man. It turned out that we were in the home of the local Lutheran minister. With fire in his eyes he told us in very loud and graphic terms what he thought of us and our church and where we were going after this life. My three days of German were more than sufficient to understand his message. We were then ordered to get out of his house. On the front steps, after the door had been slammed, my visibly shaken companion asked me if I had understood what the man was saying. I told Elder Reading that no translation was necessary!

The next several days were difficult for me. I had come to the realization that the two and a half years would be spent tracting nine or more hours per day with almost no success in terms of baptisms. Questions started bothering me. Why weren't we sent to the Southern California area where we heard they were baptizing people every week? Was our church really true? Could our teachings stand the test of careful comparison with the Bible? I had to know for certain in order to tract for the next two and a half years and repeatedly tell the people the gospel is true. I had to be sure so I determined to do just that: to compare our church with the Bible.

It wasn't long before Elder Reading and I started having a few discussions with people about The Church of Jesus Christ of Latter-day Saints. These were marvelous opportunities for me to compare the Church with what other people said and with the scriptures. I will never forget how, as we told a certain lady the story of the Book of Mormon, she became very incensed that we thought there could be other scriptures than the Bible. She turned to the last verse of the last chapter in the last book of the New Testament and read John's statement that no man may add to the things which are written in this book. (Rev. 22:18-19.) I almost died. She had us. It said so right there in black and white.

To my surprise Elder Reading did not panic, or even seem concerned. He smiled a friendly smile and started asking the woman questions. She admitted that the New Testament was made up of writings from a number of inspired men such as Peter, Paul, John, and Mark. My companion then asked her if she believed all of the books of the New Testament and accepted them as scripture. She said she did. He agreed and then asked specifically about the Gospel of John. Yes, she certainly accepted it. A short discussion then followed about who was the author of the book of Revelations. It was agreed that John, the same John who wrote the Gospel of John, wrote the Book of Revelations.

With all these preliminary points agreed to, my companion asked the lady if she knew the dates when the Gospel of John and the Book of Revelations were written. She said that she was not sure. Elder Reading turned to the back of his Bible and showed the investigator a table which indicated who wrote each of the books in the New Testament and when they were written. It showed that the Apostle John wrote the Book of Revelations in 69 A.D., and that he wrote his Gospel of John between 85 and 90 A.D. This meant that the admonition at the end of the Book of Revelations must pertain only to that Book, not to the whole New Testament, since the Gospel of John was written years after the Book of Revelations. My companion went on to show in Amos 3:7 that the Lord always works through his prophets. He then ended with his testimony that we have living prophets and continuing revelation and scripture even today. I was impressed. My testimony had been strengthened.

In the following weeks, as Elder Reading and I carefully studied the scriptures, this example of having a question and then finding the answer was repeated many times over. My understanding of how our Savior's Church had been organized and what were its basic teachings became much clearer. Comparing Jesus Christ's Church with today's religions, and with our own restored church, significantly strengthened my testimony of the divinity of The Church of Jesus Christ of Latter-day Saints. Time and time again I found myself saying, "What our church says is completely consistent." Through this whole process an increasing enthusiasm grew within me for being a missionary. I wanted to testify to other people that the fulness of the gospel had been restored. As a new missionary, studying the gospel certainly strengthened my own testimony and personal spirituality.

Why do so many missionaries feel the Spirit of the Lord while on their missions? Why do they receive direction and help through the Holy Ghost? There are several reasons including the missionaries' keeping the commandments, serving the Lord, fervently praying, and the importance of the work they are doing. It also has to do with their studying the gospel every day. By studying they learn and are reminded of why the Church is truly what we proclaim it to be; the true and everlasting gospel restored to the earth in its fulness.

Study Charges Our Batteries

As church leaders, we also need to learn and be reminded of why our church is really the restored gospel of Jesus Christ. Having once had a particularly spiritual experience, or a clear understanding of gospel principles, does not guarantee that our personal spirituality will remain strong for the rest of our lives. Such experiences and understandings act as powerful sources of energy which fill us with the Spirit just as an electric current charges a battery. But even the best batteries will become drained of energy and life if they are not periodically recharged. As church leaders, we must keep our batteries charged with personal spirituality if we are to become that malleable pure clay in the Potter's hands. One of the best ways to achieve this is through continual gospel study. Then the Master Craftsman can use us in accomplishing His greatest of all works; that of bringing to pass the immortality and eternal life of man.

Through the pages of this book we have discussed a number of leadership and church government principles and practices which can make significant positive differences in lengthening our leadership stride. Many of these are methods and ideas which have been highly successful for LDS Church leaders. As such, they form the walls, ceilings, doors and roof of our finely constructed leadership house and are very important to our eventual goal of a completely built home. As we now strive to lengthen our steps in positions of responsibility, let us not lose track of the most important leadership qualities we need for success. Building a second story window is important as long as we keep in mind the most critical and important part of the building: the foundation. The larger and weightier the finished house, the greater the need for a solid foundation. We must continually strengthen our own foundation of personal spirituality through repentance, obedience, prayer, and gospel study. By so doing we will become fine clay in the Master's hands, and successful in positions of leadership in the Church.

Index